Quick Clicks
REFERENCE GUIDE

D0060628

MICROSOFT®
WORD®
2010

CAREERTRACK®

QuickClicks Word 2010 Reference Guide

First Edition

Litho U.S.A.

Distributed in the U.S. and Canada

For orders or more information, please contact our customer service department at 1-800-556-3009.

ISBN: 978-1-60959-039-0

Item #32019

Trademarks

Disclaimer

Purchasers, readers, or users of this book agree to be bound by the following terms:

Information contained in this book has been obtained by CareerTrack from sources believed to be reliable. The subject matter of this book is constantly evolving, and the information provided in this book is not exhaustive. The advice and strategies contained within might not be suitable for every situation. It should not be used as a substitute for consulting with a qualified professional where professional assistance is required or appropriate, or where there may be any risk to health or property.

In no event will CareerTrack or any of its respective affiliates, distributors, employees, agents, content contributors, or licensors be liable or responsible for damages including direct, indirect, special, consequential, incidental, punitive, exemplary losses, or damages and expenses including business interruption, loss of profits, lost business, or lost savings.

For purposes of illustrating the concepts and techniques described in this book, the author has created fictitious names; mailing, e-mail, and internet addresses; phone and fax numbers; and similar information. Any resemblance of this fictitious data that is similar to an actual person or organization is unintentional and purely coincidental.

The *QuickClicks Reference Guide* series is dedicated to all of CareerTrack's devoted customers. Our customers' commitment to continuing education and professional development inspired the creation of the award-winning *Unlocking the Secrets* CD-ROM series and the *QuickClicks Reference Guide* series.

Thank you for your continued support!

Contents

Introduction

Congratulations on your purchase of *QuickClicks: Microsoft Word 2010*. You have invested wisely in yourself and taken a step forward in your personal and professional development.

This reference guide is an important tool in your productivity toolbox. By effectively using the word processing functions within Microsoft Word, you will be able to maximize your efficiency. The tips in this reference guide are written for the user who has a basic understanding of word processing and at least one year of experience using other Microsoft Office applications.

Anatomy of a Tip

Each tip displays the tip title in the top left corner and the tip category in the top right, so you always know where you are and what you are learning. Each tip is written in plain English. Some tips will include a "What Microsoft Calls It" reference to help you perform more effective searches for additional feature capabilities in Microsoft's help system.

Each tip is assigned a difficulty value from one to four, with one circle representing the easiest tips and four circles representing the hardest.

Difficulty: ●○○○

All tips begin with a business scenario, identified as **PROBLEM**.

SOLUTION explains how the demonstrated feature might be used to solve the problem. A set of easy-to-understand instructions follows.

Letter callouts, **A**, point to important parts of the screen. The names of all selections and buttons are **bolded** and easy to find.

Extras Include the Following

Icon	Name	What it Means
	Bright Idea	**Bright Ideas** provide additional information about Word or the features in question.
	Hot Tip	**Hot Tips** share related functions and features, or additional uses of the features and functions, to the one being demonstrated.
	Caution	**Cautions** draw attention to situations where you might find yourself tripped up by a particularly complicated operation, instances when making an incorrect choice will cause you more work to correct, or times when very similar options might be confusing.

There are two other bonuses that do not have miniature icons. They are displayed at the end of tips, where appropriate. These are:

Icon	Name	What it Means
	Options	**Options** represent places where there are two or more ways to accomplish a task or where two or more results might be obtained, depending on the choices you make. Option icons appear within the text and all relevant choices are next to the icon.
	Quickest Click	**Quickest Clicks** indicate there is a faster way to accomplish the same task taught in the tip. Shortcuts like this, though, may leave out important steps that help you understand the feature. Therefore, each tip teaches the most complete method for accomplishing a task, and a Microsoft Quickest Click appears if there is a faster option.

At the bottom of each page you will see either a **Continue** or a **Stop** icon. These icons indicate whether a tip continues on the next page or if it is complete.

Understanding Word 2010

Microsoft Word is a powerful, word-processing program that enables you to easily create, modify, and share documents for print, electronic, or online use. Word 2010 is more powerful than previous versions of Word because new features and a new interface have improved usability and efficiency.

Word users can produce simple documents, such as fax cover sheets, letters, and memos, as well as complex documents, such as reports, syllabi, proposals, and grant applications. Word 2010 interfaces with other Microsoft Office 2010 applications to create presentation materials (PowerPoint), personalized communication such as letters and invitations (Excel), and printed calendars and agendas (Outlook).

Word 2010 is a powerful tool for a variety of users:

Teachers or Trainers: Create educational materials for online use (with a variety of options such as active link and graphic elements) and for print (with a variety of options for sectioning the material into chapters or modules, page numbering, and formatting).

Students: Create reports and documents as well as bibliographies or works cited pages. Word 2010 provides automated formatting around standard writing styles used in most colleges and universities, including MLA and APA styles.

Managers and Team Leads: Create interactive, linked work schedules and automated Quality Monitoring Forms, or document employee performance.

Small Business Owners: Create invoices, billing schedules, and marketing materials with Word 2010's powerful design and formatting tools.

Getting Around Word 2010

Items Seen in the Word Window

Microsoft Word works similarly to most other Microsoft Office 2007 applications in terms of window structure and basic functions.

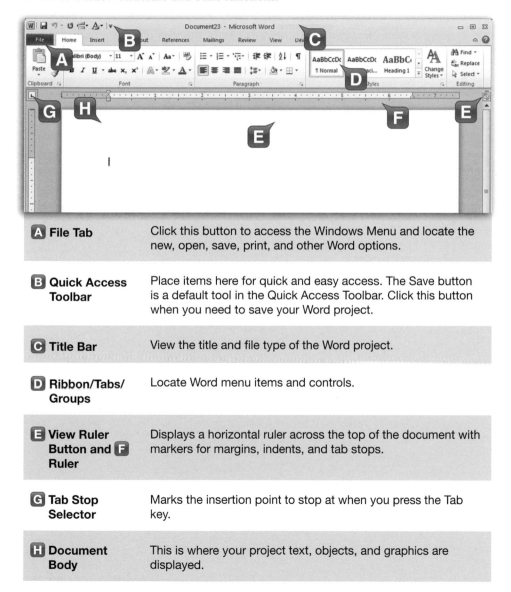

A File Tab	Click this button to access the Windows Menu and locate the new, open, save, print, and other Word options.	
B Quick Access Toolbar	Place items here for quick and easy access. The Save button is a default tool in the Quick Access Toolbar. Click this button when you need to save your Word project.	
C Title Bar	View the title and file type of the Word project.	
D Ribbon/Tabs/ Groups	Locate Word menu items and controls.	
E View Ruler Button and F Ruler	Displays a horizontal ruler across the top of the document with markers for margins, indents, and tab stops.	
G Tab Stop Selector	Marks the insertion point to stop at when you press the Tab key.	
H Document Body	This is where your project text, objects, and graphics are displayed.	

I Status Bar	The Status Bar is located at the bottom of the Word window and contains information such as page count, word count, view buttons, and a Zoom Slider.
J Document View Shortcut Buttons	Click to toggle between print layout, full screen, Web layout, outline and draft view.
K Zoom Slider	Zoom is the display size of a document within the document window. A higher zoom percentage (300%) makes everything appear larger, while a lower zoom percentage (50%) makes everything smaller. Use the plus and minus buttons to increase and decrease zoom.
L Browse By button	The Select Browse Object button brings up a menu that allows users to browse through the document by element or object type, including–for example–pages, headings, comments, footnotes, fields and search (find) terms.
M Previous/ **N** Next buttons	Click the **Previous** button to view the last object in the Document. Click the **Next** button to view the next object in the Document. You will move between the kind of object you have selected from the Select Browse Object menu. Default is page.

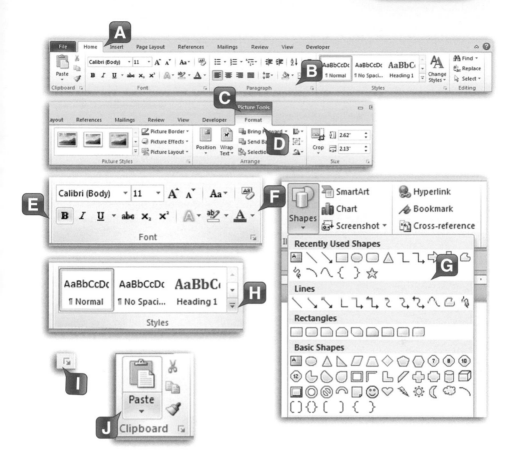

Items You'll See on the Ribbon

A Tab	Collections of related features and functions.	
B Group	Collections of related controls.	
C Highlighted Ribbon Section	Contextual ribbon sections appear when some objects are selected or used.	
D Contextual Tabs	Some specialized tabs only appear when a particular feature is active. These special tabs usually appear in conjunction with a highlighted ribbon section.	
E Button	Buttons are single-click controls that perform one function.	
F Dropdown Menus and Dropdown Buttons	Some buttons have a graphic and a down-pointing arrow, while others have a default selection visible, followed by a down arrow. Clicking the arrow reveals additional choices.	
G Selection Box	A panel containing a list of selectable items.	
H Panel Launcher or More button	A scroll control that can be clicked to launch a selection panel.	
I Dialog Box Launcher	A special group control that launches a related dialog box.	
J Combo Button	These controls are split into two parts to function as both a button and a dropdown. They may be split horizontally or vertically.	

Note: The Ribbon changes depending on your screen size, window size, and resolution. A small window might display only icons on the Ribbon **K**, whereas a large window might display the full text for each button and option **L**. The images shown in this book might look different from what you see on your own screen. However, icons will always remain consistent and the group names and placements will be the same (unless you have customized your Ribbon).

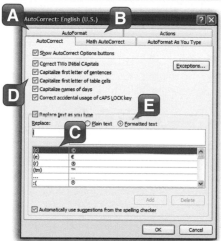

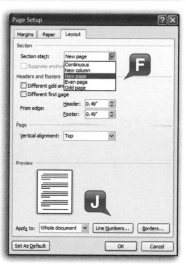

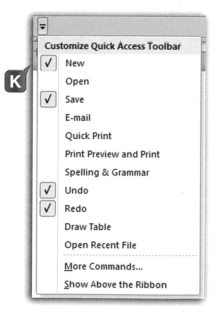

A Dialog Box	A feature-specific box that you can launch to control various functions in Excel.	
B Tabs	Some dialog boxes have tabs similar to the one on the ribbon. Each tab is focused on a particular subset of features.	
C Textbox	A box where text can be typed.	
D Checkbox	A box that activates the related selection when checked and deactivates it when unchecked. More than one checkbox may be checked in a series.	
E Radio Button	A circle that activates the related selection when selected and deactivates it when deselected. Only one radio button may be selected in a series.	
F Dropdown Menu	A simple down-pointing arrow button that reveals a set of selectable choices.	
G Right-Click Menu	This two-part menu appears when you right-click anywhere on the sheet.	
H Dialog Box Launcher	In menus, buttons that launch dialog boxes are followed by ellipses (...)..	
I Menu Launcher	Menu selections that open additional menus are followed by right-pointing arrows.	
J Shortcut Keys	Menu selections that can be launched by a keystroke on your keyboard are identified by the underlined letters in them. Click any underlined letter in a menu to launch that selection's function.	
J Toggle Checkmarks	Some menus have checkmarks. Clicking an unchecked item in those lists checks it and activates the selected option. Clicking a checked item unchecks it and deactivates the selected option.	

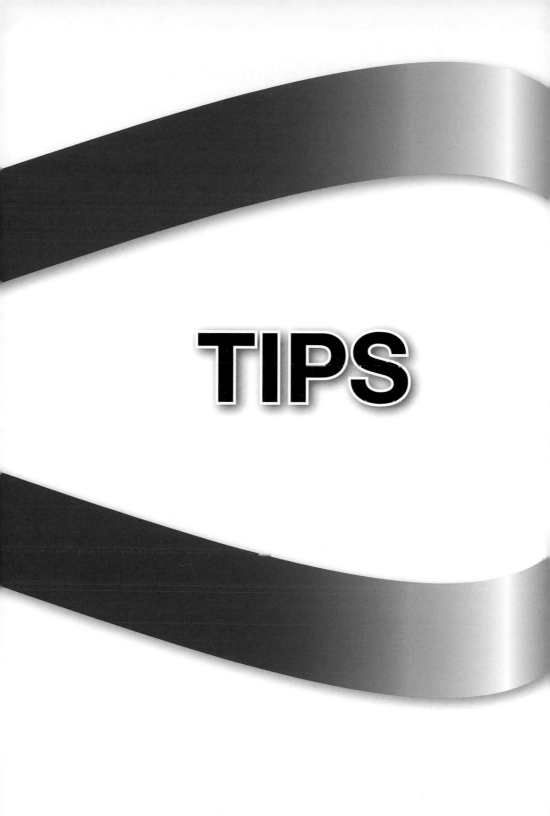

1 Customize Your Word Environment

Difficulty: ●○○○

PROBLEM There are several actions and commands you use frequently, but they are spread across multiple tabs and often several clicks deep. It would be helpful if they were more accessible to match your personal work style or the needs of your business.

SOLUTION Because Word is designed to enhance productivity, Microsoft has provided ways for organizations and users to customize their workspaces and experience.

Some customization is achieved by adding options to the **Quick Access Toolbar** or the **Status Bar**, but the most robust changes are accessible from the **Word Options** dialog box.

>  **What Microsoft Calls It:** Customize User Preferences

See Also: Customize your Word Window, Customize the Quick Access Toolbar, and Customize the Ribbon

Step-by-Step

Set User Preferences in Word

1. Click the **File** tab **A**.

2. Click the Options button **B** to launch the **Word Options** dialog box.

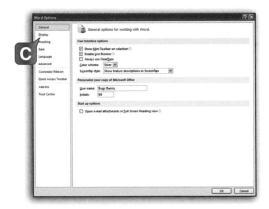

3. Click the menu tabs to view the options you want to adjust **C**:

- **General**: Change some basic defaults within Word, including user interface options, and personalize your copy of Word.

- **Display:** Change how content is displayed on the screen and when printed.

- **Proofing:** Modify how Word corrects and formats text. AutoCorrect, Spelling and Grammar preferences are set here.

- **Save:** Customize how documents are saved and how AutoRecover information is handled.

- **Language:** Choose your Office language preferences for proofing (spelling, grammar...) and Help texts.

- **Advanced:** Modify many additional Word settings, including Cut/Copy/Paste preferences, Image handling, and Editing preferences. Note that many of the settings adjusted here have ramifications that should be carefully considered before changes are made.

- **Customize Ribbon:** Add/remove or regroup items on the Ribbon.

- **Quick Access Toolbar:** Add/remove items to/from the Quick Access Toolbar.

- **Add-Ins:** Manage your Word Add-Ins. Note that most installed Add-Ins will not appear on the Add-Ins tab unless they are active.

- **Trust Center:** Manage document security settings.

4. Click the **OK** button **D**.

2 | Customize Your Word Window

Difficulty: ●○○○

PROBLEM You find yourself changing the window settings every time you open Word to fit your personal preferences. You would like to customize your Word window to default to these settings each time you open Word and begin to work.

SOLUTION Since every person uses Word in a slightly different way, **Word Options** allows you to change popular options to personalize what appears in the Word window. When you change these options, Word uses them for all Word windows you open, unless you change them.

Step-by-Step

Customize the User Interface

1. Click the **File** tab **A**.

2. Click the **Options** button **B** to launch the **Word Options** dialog box. The dialog box will open, by default, on the **General** tab **C**.

3. Choose from the **User Interface option**s section  **D** to set user interface preferences:

- **Show Mini Toolbar on Selection:** Select this option to show a miniature semi-transparent toolbar that helps you work with selected text.

- **Enable Live Preview:** Turn this option off if you do not want your document to preview changes as you hover over menu items (style, formatting, theme, etc). You might choose to turn this off when you are working through a remote connection or if your computer is very slow.

- **Always use ClearType:** ClearType is a software technology developed by Microsoft that improves the readability of text on existing LCDs and flat panel monitors. Default is checked.

- **Color scheme:** The default 2010 window color scheme is silver. Click the down arrow to choose from Blue, Silver, or Black **E**.

- **ScreenTip style:** Click the down arrow to select a screen tip option:

  o Show enhanced ScreenTips

  o Don't show enhanced ScreenTips

  o Don't show ScreenTips

4. Click **OK F** to close window and apply changes.

Step-by-Step

Change Display Settings

1. Click the **File** tab **A**.

2. Click the **Options** button **B** to launch the **Word Option**s dialog box. Click the **Display** tab **G**.

3. Select or clear any of the check boxes **H** to change the display options you want:

    - **Show white space between pages in Print Layout view:** Select this option to display top and bottom margins.

    - **Show highlighter marks:** Select this option to display highlighted text on the screen and in print.

    - **Show document tooltips on hover:** Select this option to display information when you point to a hyperlink or reviewer's comment.

4. Select or clear any of the check boxes to display or hide the formatting marks you want.

    - Tab characters, Spaces, Paragraph marks, Hidden text, Optional hyphens, or Object anchors.

    - Show all formatting marks.

5. Click **OK** **I** to close window and apply changes.

3 | Manage Your Files in the Backstage View

Difficulty: ●○○○

PROBLEM You manage several documents every week. Not only do you create new documents on a regular basis, but you also update, edit and share many existing files. You need file management tools that will help you stay organized and work more efficiently.

SOLUTION Take advantage of the features available in Word 2010's **Backstage View**.

Step-by-Step

1. Click the **File** tab  **A** to access the **Backstage** view:

   - The **Info** **B** tab will be selected by default. From the **Info** tab you can manage permissions from the **Protect Document** button **C**, compatibility options under the **Check for Issues** button **D**, and version control under the **Manage Versions** button **E**. The **Properties** pane **F** gives you file data such as size, dates modified, and author.

- Your most common tasks such as **Save**, **Save As**, **Open**, and **Close** are located at the top of the **File** menu **G**. **Exit** is located at the bottom **H**.

- The **Recent** tab **I** opens a pane that displays the most **Recent Workbooks** **J** you have opened. Recently accessed folders and file paths are displayed in the **Recent Places** pane **K**. 🔥

3 Manage Your Files in the Backstage View (continued)

- The **New** tab  is where you will open a new workbook by choosing from Excel's many built-in **Available Templates** M. More templates are available under the **Office.com Templates** N heading (internet connection required). A preview of each template will appear in the **Preview Pane** O. Click the **Create** button P to open the template you've chosen.

- The **Print** tab Q offers some of the most common print options under the **Settings** heading R, including Print Area, Pages, Collation, Orientation, Paper size, Margin settings, and Scaling. Check the **Print Preview** pane S frequently to see how your content will be displayed as you are working with it.

- The **Save & Send** tab is where you will find tools to share your documents via email, the Web, or SharePoint.

- The **Help** tab is where you can go to find answers to questions and problems you may be having.

- The **Options** tab launches the **Word Options** dialog box.

Hot Tip: Use the **Recent** tab to open files you access frequently without having to browse through many folders to find them.

If you open many documents every day, you can **Pin** your most important documents to the top of the list. Click any grey pin on the **Recent Workbooks** or **Recent Places** lists. The pin will turn blue and the file will jump to the top of the list where it will remain until you unpin it. Click the blue pin to unpin the item.

4 Browse Text and Objects in Your Document

Difficulty: ●●○○

PROBLEM You are working on a very long document. You frequently need to refer to previous sections and find specific content as you go. You would like a faster way than scrolling page by page to browse the document.

SOLUTION Use the **Navigation** pane. Word 2010 introduced the Navigation pane as a consolidated resource to move quickly through your documents.

Step-by-Step

Use the Navigation Pane

1. On the **View** tab, in the **Show** group, click the **Navigation Pane** checkbox . This will open the **Navigation** pane **B** to the left of your document pane.

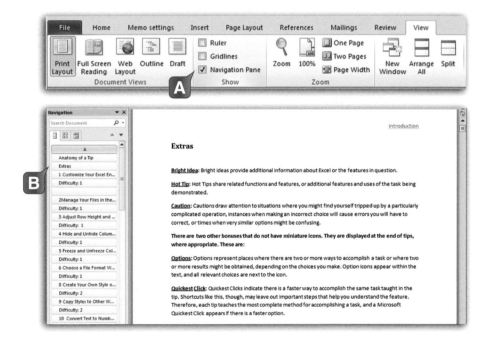

2. The **Navigation** pane contains three tabs:

Browse the headings in your document C: The pane will display a list of the document's **Heading** titles. You can jump directly to the page containing the **Heading** by clicking on the **Heading's** title. When you right-click on a **Heading**, you can choose from several tasks such as adding new **Headings** to your document and promoting or demoting **Headings** to higher or lower **Heading** levels. To move a **Heading** to a new place in your document, just click and drag it to its new spot.

CONTINUE ▶

Browse the pages in your document D: View thumbnail images of the document pages. Click on any thumbnail to take you to the page.

Browse results from your current search E: Insert a search phrase into the **Search Document** text box **F** and the results will be highlighted in the document pane and listed in the **Navigation** pane. Click any result to jump to the page.

Quickest Click: Click the **Select Browse Object** button 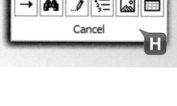G in the lower right hand corner of your Word window or press **ALT + CTRL + HOME** on your keyboard to bring up the **Select Browse** command menu H. The icons represent the following actions to browse:

- Go To
- Find
- By Edits
- By Heading
- By Graphic
- By Table
- By Field
- By Endnote
- By Footnote
- By Comment
- By Section
- By Page

Once you have selected the object you want to browse by, click the Next / Previous arrows to jump quickly from one instance of the object to the next within your document.

5 | Save a Document to the Appropriate File Format

Difficulty: ●○○○

PROBLEM The document you have been working on will need to be reviewed by collaborators who have different versions of Word. Once the document is approved, the content will need to be prepared for upload to your corporate internal Web pages. You want to save a document (or a copy of a document) that others can use and that will be in the correct format for all of its future uses..

SOLUTION Use the **Save As** command. Word offers you many options when it comes to file types and formats, each with its own purposes. Choosing the appropriate file format depends upon the technological specifications of the users of the document. It is important to know how a document will be used—who will view or edit the document, and how often it will be changed. Save your documents to the correct file type to meet the needs of those who will receive your work.dialog box.

Step-by-Step

Choose a File Format When Saving a Document

1. Click on the **File** tab **A**.

2. Click **Save As** **B**. The **Save As** dialog box **C** will pop open.

3. Type a file name for your workbook in the **File name** text box **D**.

4. Select a file type from the **Save as type**: dropdown menu **E**.

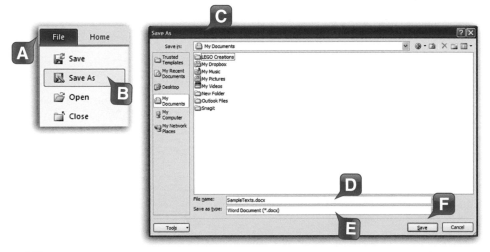

- **Word Document:** .DOCX The default format for Word 2010.

- **Word Macro-Enabled Document**: .DOCM This format is essentially the same as the default format, except that it can store macros. If you include macros, you will be prompted to save in this format. .DOTM is the template version of this format.

- **Word 97-2003 Document:** .DOC This is a format fully accessible by previous versions of Word back to 97. The .DOT format, 97-2003 template, is also available.

- **Word Template:** .DOTX The Word 2010 format for templates.

- **PDF and XPS:** .PDF and .XPS are read-only formats that will produce easy to read, share, and print documents.

- **Rich Text Format:** .RTF A generic word processing format, supported by almost all word processing programs other than Word. Retains basic features as tables and text formatting.

- **Plain Text:** .TXT This format saves the text only, with no formatting.

- **Web Page:** .HTML or .HTM A web page that retains all the coding it needs for full use in Word, in addition to all coding needed for full use on the Web. Graphics and additional files are stored in a separate folder.

- Other file types: Other formats are available such as .XML (eXtensible Markup Language) and .MHTML / .MHT (for HTML-based e-mail).

5.   Click the **Save** button **F**.

6 Adjust Line and Paragraph Spacing

Difficulty: ●○○○

PROBLEM You need to present an outline of your department's annual goals to the vice president. Your manager recommends that this presentation be one page only. The first draft of your document is more than a page. However, there is a lot of empty space that you can eliminate to reduce the document to a single page.

SOLUTION Adjust the spacing. **Line Spacing** establishes the amount of vertical space between the lines of text in a paragraph. **Paragraph Spacing** establishes the amount of space above or below a paragraph. Microsoft Word 2010 sets default line spacing at 1.15 and default paragraph spacing at 10 points. There are many instances when you may need to adjust this spacing to be larger or smaller, depending how the document will be used.

 Step-by-Step

Adjust Line Spacing

1. Highlight the text you want to adjust or press **CTRL+A** on your keyboard to select all text in the document. *Note: You can choose these settings before you type any text into your document.*

2. In the **Paragraph** group in the **Home** tab, click on the **Line Spacing** button **A**.

3. Select one of the preset spacing options available **B**. A checkmark **C** will appear by the one you have chosen.

4. For more options, click **Line Spacing Options** **D** to open the **Paragraph** dialog box and then make your selection from the **Line spacing:** dropdown **E**.

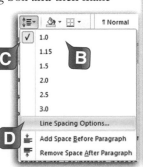

- **Single:** Alters the spacing to the largest font used in the line of text and includes a small amount of extra space. The amount of extra space varies depending on the font that is used..

> **Joseph and the Turtle**
>
> Once upon a time there was a boy who loved animals. He walked by the local pet shop every morning on his way to school. One morning while he was walking by, he noticed a new animal in the window. It was a turtle larger than the size of his head. He was amazed by what he saw. He stood in the window for a few minutes just watching the turtle. He said to himself, "I think he looks like a nice animal. I think I will stop and see him on my way home from school." And that is just what he did.

- **1.5 lines:** One and one-half times single line spacing.

> **Joseph and the Turtle**
>
> Once upon a time there was a boy who loved animals. He walked by the local
>
> pet shop every morning on his way to school. One morning while he was
>
> walking by, he noticed a new animal in the window. It was a turtle larger than
>
> the size of his head. He was amazed by what he saw. He stood in the window for
>
> a few minutes just watching the turtle. He said to himself, "I think he looks like a
>
> nice animal. I think I will stop and see him on my way home from school." And a

- **Double:** Twice the size of single line spacing.

> **Joseph and the Turtle**
>
> Once upon a time there was a boy who loved animals. He walked by the local
>
> pet shop every morning on his way to school. One morning while he was
>
> walking by, he noticed a new animal in the window. It was a turtle larger than
>
> the size of his head. He was amazed by what he saw. He stood in the window for
>
> a few minutes just watching the turtle. He said to himself, "I think he looks like a
>
> nice animal. I think I will stop and see him on my way home from school." And a

- **At least:** Sets the minimum line spacing needed to fit the largest font or graphic in that line of text.

- **Exactly:** Sets fixed line spacing, expressed in font points. For instance, if the text is in a 14-point font, you can specify 20-points as the line spacing.

- Sets line spacing relative to the current font. For instance, setting line spacing to 3 increases the space by 300%. This is the setting that is changed when you choose a preset number from the Line Spacing button **A** in the Paragraph group

Step-by-Step

Adjust Paragraph Spacing

1. Highlight the paragraph for which you wish to adjust the spacing.

2. In the **Paragraph** group on the **Page Layout** tab, click the arrow next to **Spacing Before E** or **Spacing After F** to adjust the spacing, or type the amount of space required in the text box **G**.

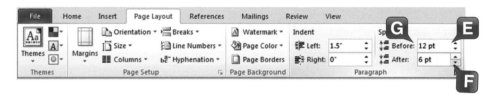

Step-by-Step

Widows and Orphans

A widow occurs when the last line of a paragraph appears by itself at the top of a new page. An orphan is the first line of a paragraph by itself at the bottom of a page. You can use the Widow/Orphan Control option to automatically keep paragraph text together. If a line is widowed or orphaned, Word adjusts the paragraph to make sure at least two lines appear together on the next page. This setting can be applied to selected paragraphs (as described below) or can be applied to the document as a whole.

1. Select the paragraph you want to keep together.

2. Click the dialog box launcher **H** in the bottom-right corner of the **Paragraph** group on the **Home** tab.

3. Click the **Line and Page Breaks** tab **I** in the **Paragraph** dialog box.

4. Choose an option from the **Pagination** settings:

- **Widow/Orphan control:** Select this check box to avoid paragraphs ending with a single word on a line or a single line at the top of a page **J**.

- **Keep with next:** Select this check box to group paragraphs together **K**.

- **Keep lines together:** Select this check box to keep paragraph lines together **L**.

- **Page break before:** Select this check box to precede a paragraph with a page break **M**.

5. Click **OK** to apply changes **N**.

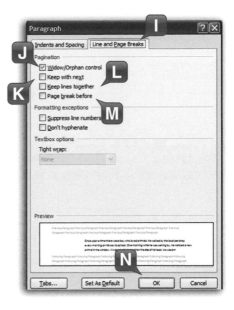

Bright Idea: If you use the same settings repeatedly, create a template with those settings OR a macro to adjust the settings to your standard layout. You can also change line spacing for an entire document by using Styles. In the **Styles** group on the **Home** tab, click the **Change Styles** button **O**. Hover over **Style Set** **P** or **Paragraph Spacing** **Q** to preview various spacing styles.

Caution: Line and paragraph spacing information is stored "in" the paragraph mark at the end of a line. You must include this paragraph marker ¶ in your selection to be sure your changes apply to the appropriate text. Click the **Paragraph** button **R** in the **Paragraph** group of the **Home** tab to reveal these symbols.

7 | Adjust Text Alignment and Tabs

Difficulty: ●○○○

PROBLEM You want to emphasize the title of a document or a portion of a document by centering the text so that the reader's eyes are drawn to it. In addition, you want to line up your text along a margin to make the presentation neat and symmetrical.

SOLUTION Text alignment determines the appearance and orientation of the edges of the paragraph. These options are left-aligned, right-aligned, centered, and justified. These elements can be used for both space and document design purposes.

Tab stops enable you to line up text to the left, right, center, or to a decimal character. You can insert specific characters, such as periods or dashes, before the tabs.

Step-by-Step

Text Alignment

1. Select the text to be aligned.

2. In the **Paragraph** group **A** on the **Home** tab, click the desired alignment for the text from the options: **B**

- **Align Left**: Aligns all selected text to the left margin **C**.

> When attending a baseball game, it's important to remember why people are there. First, there's the game. The pureness of baseball - the balls, the bats; the diamond; the dirt –RBIs and home runs –it's a true miracle for a true baseball fan. Second, there's the experience. The people yelling. The baseball hats. The vulgarity (it happens) and the smell. You know who you are. The smell of the baseball game …it's something most can only dream of. And lastly, there's the grub. The beer, the peanuts, the cracker jacks and the dogs. Need I say more?

- **Align Right**: Aligns all selected text to the right margin .

When attending a baseball game, it's important to remember why people are there. First, there's the game. The pureness of baseball - the balls, the bats; the diamond; the dirt –RBIs and home runs –it's a true miracle for a true baseball fan. Second, there's the experience. The people yelling. The baseball hats. The vulgarity (it happens) and the smell. You know who you are. The smell of the baseball game …it's something most can only dream of. And lastly, there's the grub. The beer, the peanuts, the cracker jacks and the dogs. Need I say more?

- **Center**: Centers all selected text between the margins .

When attending a baseball game, it's important to remember why people are there. First, there's the game. The pureness of baseball - the balls, the bats; the diamond; the dirt –RBIs and home runs –it's a true miracle for a true baseball fan. Second, there's the experience. The people yelling. The baseball hats. The vulgarity (it happens) and the smell. You know who you are. The smell of the baseball game …it's something most can only dream of. And lastly, there's the grub. The beer, the peanuts, the cracker jacks and the dogs. Need I say more?

- **Justify**: Aligns all selected text evenly along the left and right margins. The last line of text in a paragraph may be shorter than the other lines .

When attending a baseball game, it's important to remember why people are there. First, there's the game. The pureness of baseball - the balls, the bats; the diamond; the dirt –RBIs and home runs –it's a true miracle for a true baseball fan. Second, there's the experience. The people yelling. The baseball hats. The vulgarity (it happens) and the smell. You know who you are. The smell of the baseball game …it's something most can only dream of. And lastly, there's the grub. The beer, the peanuts, the cracker jacks and the dogs. Need I say more?

Set Tab Stops

1. Find the horizontal ruler that runs along the top of the document. If you do not see the ruler, click the **View Ruler** button **G** at the top of the vertical scroll bar or click the **Ruler** box **H** in the **Show** group on the **View** tab.

2. Set tabs by clicking the tab selector at the left end of the ruler **I** to toggle through the tab options until it displays the type of tab you want.

- **Left Tab Stop**: Sets the start position of text that will run to the right as you type.

- **Center Tab Stop**: Sets the position of the middle of the text. The text centers on this position as you type.

- **Right Tab Stop**: Sets the right end of the text. As you type, the text moves to the left.

- **Decimal Tab Stop**: Aligns numbers around a decimal point. No matter how many numbers are used, the decimal point will stay in the same position. You cannot use the decimal tab to align numbers around any other character.

- **Bar Tab Stop**: This type of tab stop does not position text. When a bar stop is set at a particular position, pressing **Tab** to move to that spot places a vertical line the same height as that line of text. When several **Bar Stops** appear in consecutive lines, they form a solid vertical divider line, making the tabbed list resemble a table.

8 | Adjust Document Margins

Difficulty: ●○○○

PROBLEM You are sending a Press Release to an industry newsletter that requires specific format settings for all submissions. The default margin settings for Word documents do not meet these requirements.

SOLUTION Adjust your document's margins. Margins are the blank spaces between the edge of a page and the text. The default setting for Word documents is 1 inch on the left and right and 1 inch on the top and bottom. You can use the Ribbon to select preset margin options, or you can use the Page Setup dialog box to define custom margins.

Step-by-Step

Adjust Margins

1. On the **Page Layout** tab, in the **Page Setup** group, click the **Margins** button **A** to open the preset margin dropdown menu **B**. ⚠

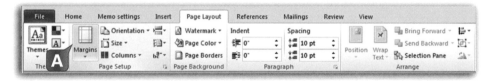

2. Click the preset margin type you want:
   - **Normal:** Default setting for Word 2010.
   - **Narrow:** Very thin margins, more room for content.
   - **Moderate:** Top margin is same as default, left and right margins are slightly smaller.
   - **Wide:** Top margin is same as default, left and right margins are double the default left and right setting.

- **Mirrored:** Use for double-sided documents such as books or magazines where you need different margin settings depending on whether the page will appear on the left or right of your final document. That is, inside margins will be the same width on the left page as it is on the right and outside margins will be the same width on the left page as it is on the right.

- **Office 2003 Default:** Those familiar with older versions of Word may use this to match the older default.

3. To create a custom margin setting, click **Custom Margins** C to open the **Page Setup** dialog box.

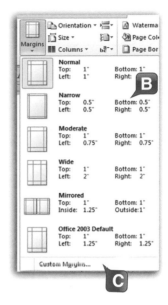

4. On the **Margins** tab of the **Page Setup** dialog box, type your margin measurements in inches in the **Top, Bottom, Left,** or **Right** text boxes 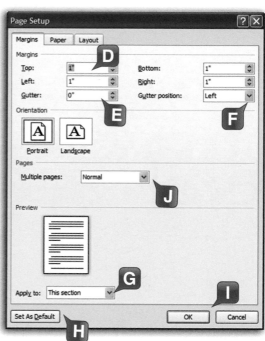.

5. To add a custom gutter margin, type a measurement into the **Gutter** text box **E** and choose the position of the gutter in the **Gutter position** dropdown box **F**.

6. Click the **Apply to** dropdown arrow **G** and select how you want your changes applied:

   - **Selected Text:** Will only apply the new margin settings to text that has been highlighted. Word will automatically insert a section break before and after the selection.

   - **Selected Sections:** Will apply the new margin settings to any document sections that currently contain selected text. The entire section or sections will be affected.

   - **This Section:** Will only apply the new margin settings to the section that you are currently working in.

   - **This Point Forward:** Automatically inserts a section break at the place where your cursor is resting and applies the new margin settings to the rest of the document from that point forward, including later section breaks.

   - **Whole Document:** Applies the new margin settings to the entire document, including all section breaks.

7. To make new margin settings the default for all new Word documents, click **Set As Default** **H** and click **Yes** at the confirmation prompt. If you are working from a template, the margin default will be changed for all new documents based on that template.

8. Click **OK** **I** to apply settings.

Caution: If your document contains multiple sections, the preset margin types will only apply to the section you are currently working in. To choose a preset margin type for multiple sections, click and drag to select the sections you want to adjust, then choose your margin type.

Quickest Click: Gutters allow for additional margin space so that all the document text remains visible after binding. To set the gutters for normal binding, display the **Margins** tab in the **Page Setup** dialog box. Click the **Multiple Pages** dropdown arrow **J** and click **Book Fold** **K**.

9 | Arrange Text in Columns

Difficulty: ●●●○

PROBLEM You want to create a one-page newsletter. Arranging your text in a normal one-column manner on your page pushes the text onto a second page. You have enough white space to add columns and make your one-page newsletter look neat and professional.

SOLUTION Columns allow you to divide a page or area of text vertically into two or more sections. The ability to arrange text in columns is particularly useful for newspaper style documents such as newsletters, training materials, and flyers.

Step-by-Step

Add Columns

1. Position the cursor where you would like columnar formatting to begin.

2. On the **Page Layout** tab in the **Page Setup** group, click the **Columns** button .

3. From the dropdown menu, select the number of columns **B** to insert into the document.

4. Word automatically inserts the columns into your document. 💧

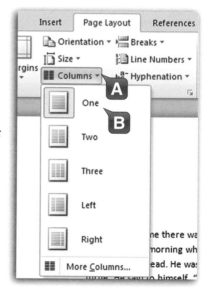

Step-by-Step

Insert a Column Break

You may decide that you would like one column shorter than the other. This can be done easily by inserting a column break.

1. Position your cursor where you would like to insert the column break.

2. On the **Page Layout** tab, in the **Page Setup** group, click the **Breaks** button **C**.

3. From the dropdown menu, select **Column D**.

4. Any text typed will begin in the next column. If there is already text following the cursor, it will be moved to the next column.

Step-by-Step

Insert a Continuous Section Break

You may not want the entire page to contain columns. In that case, insert a continuous section break in your document. You can insert one before and one after the content that contains columns.

1. Place your cursor where you want the first break.

2. On the **Page Layout** tab, in the **Page Setup** group, click the **Breaks** button **E**.

3. From the dropdown menu, click **Continuous** **F**.

Hot Tip: You can edit the spacing of individual columns to fit the needs of the document by disabling the **Equal Column Width** check-box **G** and setting your own column widths. On the **Page Layout** tab, in the page setup group, click **Columns** and select **More Columns** **H** to launch the **Columns** dialog box. If you want a vertical line to appear between the columns, select the **Line Between** check-box **I**. The line is black, fixed width, and cannot be edited.

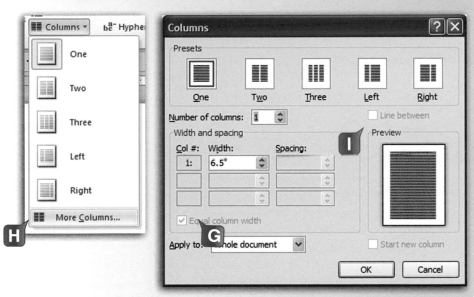

Bright Idea: You can apply separate page setup formatting — such as colors, shading, margins or borders -to individual sections of your document.

STOP

10 Apply Borders and Shading to Text or a Page

Difficulty: ●●○○

PROBLEM You are launching a new dress code policy for your company. To make it more appealing to employees, you want to create a page border and background shading that attracts the eye and showcase the images of proper attire on the page. To maintain a consistent artistic style, you want to place a border around the policy and change the color to make it stand out.

SOLUTION **Borders** are lines or graphics that appear around a page, paragraph, selected text, or table cells. With borders, you can change the line style, width, and colors or add special effects, such as shadows and 3D elements. **Shading** is a color that fills the background of selected text, paragraphs, or table cells.

Step-by-Step

1. Select the text where a border and/or shading is desired. To apply settings to a whole page, click anywhere on the page.

2. On the **Page Layout** tab, in the **Page Background** group, select **Page Borders** **A** to launch the **Borders and Shading** dialog box **B**.

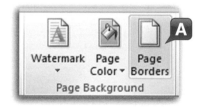

3. In the **Borders and Shading** dialog box, on the same **Page Border** tab 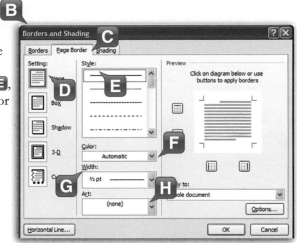, select a **Setting**, **Style**, **Color**, **Width**, and/or **Art** (includes a picture-based border instead of a line-based border).

   a. To apply settings to text only, set options on the **Page Border** tab of the dialog box.

   b. To apply settings to text only, set options on the **Borders** tab of the dialog box.

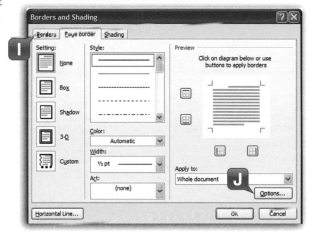

4. Select **Text**, **Paragraph**, or **Whole Document** in the **Apply to** box **J**. 🔥

5. Click the **Shading** tab **K** and select the fill color and/or patterns to apply.

6. Select **Text**, **Paragraph** or **Whole Document** in the **Apply to** drop down.

7. Click **OK L** to apply the formatting.

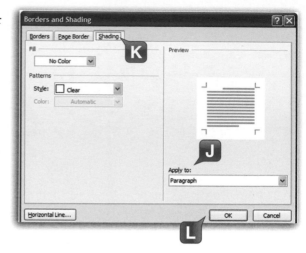

Hot Tip: If you select text from the beginning of a line to the end of a paragraph ¶ and select paragraph  in the **Apply to** dropdown, it will put a box around the whole paragraph, like this:

Apply to:

Paragraph

Text
Paragraph

Joseph and the Turtle

Once upon a time there was a boy who loved animals. He walked by the local pet shop every morning on his way to school. One morning while he was walking by, he noticed a new animal in the window. It was a turtle larger than the size of his head. He was amazed by what he saw. He stood in the window for a few minutes just watching the turtle. He said to himself, "I think he looks like a nice animal. I think I will stop and see him on my way home from school." And that is exactly what he did.

Conversely, if you select a paragraph fragment and select **Text** from the **Apply to** dropdown, it will put a box only around the selected text:

Joseph and the Turtle

Once upon a time there was a boy who loved animals. He walked by the local pet shop every morning on his way to school. One morning while he was walking by, he noticed a new animal in the window. It was a turtle larger than the size of his head. He was amazed by what he saw. He stood in the window for a few minutes just watching the turtle. He said to himself, "I think he looks like a nice animal. I think I will stop and see him on my way home from school." And that is exactly what he did.

STOP

11 | Insert a Numbered or Bulleted List

Difficulty: ●○○○

PROBLEM Your text includes a list that sits amidst paragraphs of text. You want to make the list stand out from the rest of the text, making it easier to work with and read.

SOLUTION Use a numbered or bulleted list. Lists help break text into manageable chunks.

Step-by-Step

There are two ways to approach creating a list. First you can type the entire list, select the text and then click the **Bullets A** or **Numbering B** button. Second, you can click one of the list buttons first and then type. Each time you press **Enter**, a new bullet or number is created. Pressing **Enter** at a blank bullet or number returns you to regular formatting.

1. Place cursor in the position where your list should begin.

2. On the **Home** tab, in the **Paragraph** group, click the **Bullets A** or the **Numbering B** button. 💡

3. The first bullet or number character will appear in the document.

4. Type your first item, then press **Enter**.

Normal List	Bulleted List	Numbered List
Item One	• Item One	1. Item One
Item Two	• Item Two	2. Item Two
Item Three	• Item Three	3. Item Three
Item Four	• Item Four	4. Item Four

Step-by-Step

Change Bullet or Number Styles

1. Select the list you wish to change.

2. Click the dropdown arrow on the **Bullets** or **Numbering** combo button **C** in the **Paragraph** group on the **Home** tab.

3. Select a predefined bullet or number style **D** from the dropdown menu.

4. To choose from more bullet options or to customize your bullet graphics, click **Define New Bullet E** or **Define New Number Format F** to launch the **Define New Bullet** or **Define Number Format** dialog box

5. For bullets, click **Symbol G** to open the **Symbol** dialog box, or **Picture H** to open the **Picture Bullet** dialog box. Similar options are available in the **Define Number Format** box.

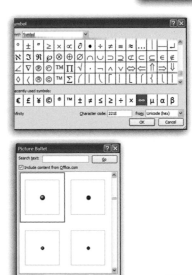

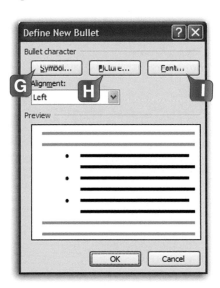

CONTINUE

6. If needed, specify the font style/size and alignment by clicking the **Font** button in the **Define New Bullet** dialog box to open the **Font** dialog box.

7. Click **OK** to apply changes.

Bulleted List Using Symbols	Bulleted List Using Pictures
∞ Item One	🔘 Item One
∞ Item Two	🔘 Item Two
∞ Item Three	🔘 Item Three
∞ Item Four	🔘 Item Four

Step-by-Step

Create a Multi-Level Bulleted or Numbered List/Outline

1. Begin typing your list using either bullets or numbers.

2. At the position you want to indent to the next level, press **Tab**.

3. Type your text and press **Enter**.

4. Press **Shift+Tab** to return to the previous level bullet or number.

Multi-Level Bulleted List	Multi-Level Numbered List
• Item One	1. Item One
o Item One–A	a. Item One–A
o Item One–B	b. Item One–B
• Item Two	2. Item Two
o Item Two–A	a. Item Two–A
o Item Two–B	b. Item Two–B

Quickest Click: To return to the previous level in your list for the next item, click **Enter** multiple times until you go back to the desired level.

 Hot Tip: To format the list type, select the list, click the **Multi-Level List** button on the **Home** tab and select a format.

 Bright Idea: Quickly create a numbered list by following these easy steps:
1. Place your cursor where you want to begin the list.
2. Type **1**.
3. Press the **Spacebar** and enter your text. AutoFormat will begin a numbered list for you and display the **Autocorrect** symbol .
4. Press **Enter** to continue the numbering.
5. Press **Enter** and **Backspace** to end the list.

 Caution: If you are creating a list in a Table, use the **Increase Indent** button **K** in the **Paragraph** group on the **Home** tab to create the next level in your list or the **Decrease Indent** button **L** to return to the previous level.

12 | Format Your Text

Difficulty:

PROBLEM You are pleased with the content and organization of your document and are ready to make it more visually appealing.

SOLUTION Format your text. Formatting can be applied to individual characters, words, phrases, paragraphs, whole pages, or documents. Options include font (or typeface, such as Arial or Times New Roman), font characteristics (such as bold, italics), size, color, and effects.

Step-by-Step

Change Font Typeface and Size

1. Place your cursor in the document at the place you want the new font setting to begin, or select the text to which the change will be applied.

2. In the **Font** group on the **Home** tab, the current font **A** and size **B** will be displayed. Click the dropdown arrow to open the font **C** or font size **D** menus.

   Theme Fonts E, those fonts associated with the theme your document is using, will be displayed at the top of the **Font Menu**.

   Preview the changes before you make your selection by hovering over the new font typeface **F** or point size **G**.

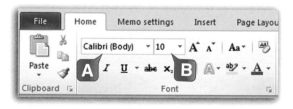

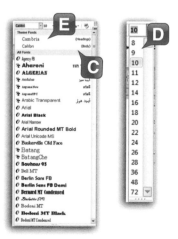

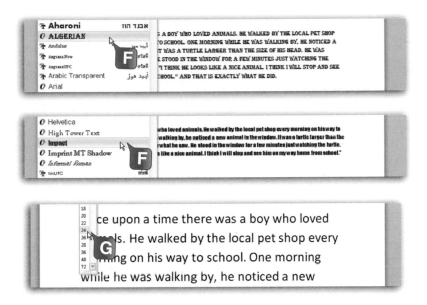

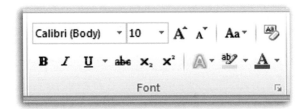

3. Click the font typeface or font size you want to apply the changes.

Step-by-Step

Add Font Styles and Effects

1. Select the text you want to change.

2. Click the **Style** or **Effect** you want to apply to your text from the **Font** group:

Bold	**B**
Italicize	*I*
<u>Underline</u>	U ▾ More Underlines... Underline Color ▸
~~Strikethrough~~	abc
Subscript (H_2SO_4)	x_2
Superscript (Microsoft® Word®)	x^2
cHANGE cASE	Aa ▾ Sentence case. lowercase UPPERCASE Capitalize Each Word tOGGLE cASE
TEXT EFFECTS – A visual effect such as shadow, glow, or reflection	A A A A A A A A A A A A A A A A A A A A Outline ▸ Shadow ▸ Reflection ▸ Glow ▸

Text Highlight Color – Makes text look like it was marked with a highlighter pen	
Font Color – Change the color of the font itself	
Clear Formatting – Removes all formatting from the selected text	

 Quickest Click: To increase or decrease a font size a point increment at a time, click the **Grow Font H** button or **Shrink Font I** button.

 Quickest Click: Copy Formatting – Select the text with the formatting you want to copy, then click the **Format Painter** button **J** in the **Clipboard** group on the **Home** tab. Apply the copied formatting by selecting the text you want formatted. Double-click the **Format Painter** button to apply the copied formatting to multiple selections of text. Click on **Format Painter** again to end copy formatting.

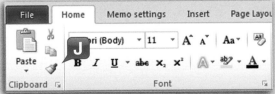

13 | Apply Styles to Text

Difficulty: ●●○○

PROBLEM You are preparing a report with many section headings. Each time you begin a new section or subsection, you have to highlight the text, change the font to Cambria and change the font size to 16-point, and click the bold button. You would like an easier way to format each heading, etc. without having to highlight the text and change the formatting each time you type a section heading.

SOLUTION Use **Styles** to format your document. A **Style** is a combination of formatting characteristics such as font, font size, paragraph alignment, and indentation that you name and store as a set. Some styles sets may also include borders and shading. Instead of making three changes to each heading, click the Heading 1 style and apply all the format changes at once.

Different style sets can then contain different combinations of formatting characteristics for a completely different look and feel for your document.

Heading 1 in the Default (Black and White) Style set

 Step-by-Step

---

Apply a Quick Style

Microsoft Word provides pre-designed **Quick Styles** for easy selection. These sets include a Normal style for body text and a variety of styles for lists, quotes, references, and text that you want to emphasize or highlight within the document.

1. Select the text you want to format.

2. On the **Home** tab, in the **Styles** group, click the **Up and Down** arrows **A** to scroll through the **QuickStyles** gallery, or click the **More** dropdown arrow **B** to expand the **QuickStyles** gallery to view more styles at a time.

3. Click a **Style** **C** to apply to your text.

CONTINUE

Step-by-Step

Change to a Different Style Set

1. On the **Home** tab, in the **Styles** group, click the **Change Styles** button 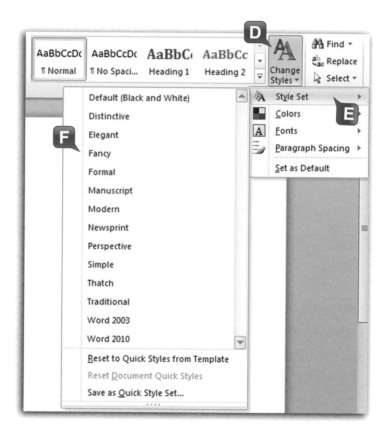.

2. Select **Style Set**, then choose from the style options in the fly out menu.

Preview the changes  **G** before you make your choice so you can see how each **Style** set will affect your content.

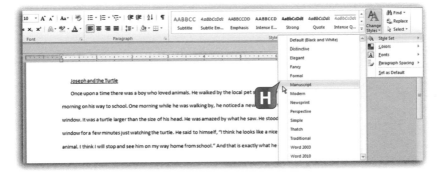

3. Click the **Style** set **H** you want to apply to your document.

Hot Tip: Using **Styles** makes creating a Table of Contents easy, as **Heading Levels** are used as Table of Contents entries. See Tip 36 on page 128 for detailed instructions.

STOP

14 | Create Your Own Style Sets and Quick Styles

Difficulty: ●●●○

PROBLEM You prepare a Status Report every week with a specific set of styles and text formatting. You would like a way to add your custom style to each new report without having to change individual settings every time.

SOLUTION Create a new **Style**. Word provides a variety of styles to choose from. However, sometimes you need to create a new style or modify an existing one to get exactly the appearance you want. You can create a paragraph or character style. A paragraph style is a group of format settings applied to all of the text within a paragraph. A character style is a group of format settings applied to any block of text that a user selects.

 Step-by-Step

Create a Style Set

1. Format a document with the style that you want to save.

2. On the **Home** tab, in the **Styles** group, click the **Change Styles** button **A**.

3. Select **Style Set B**.

4. Click **Save as Quick Style Set C** to open the **Save Quick Style Set** dialog box.

5. Type a name for your **Style Set** in the **File name:** textbox 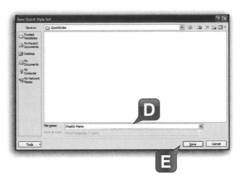.

6. Click **Save** **E**. Your custom style set will now be available from the **Change Styles** dropdown menu in any document you open. 🔥

Step-by-Step

Create a New Style or Quick Style

1. Select the specific text with the formatting you want to save.

2. On the **Home** tab, in the **Styles** group, click the **More** dropdown arrow **F** to open the **Quick Styles** gallery.

3. Select **Save Selection as a New Quick Style** **G** to launch the **Create New Style from Formatting** dialog box.

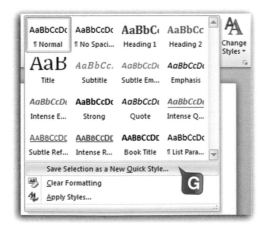

4. Type a short, descriptive name for the new style .

5. Click **Modify** .

6. Click the **Style type** dropdown arrow and choose from among the style type options:
   - **Paragraph** style can include every kind of formatting that a character style can contain, but it also can control all aspects of a paragraph's appearance such as text alignment, tab stops, line spacing, margins, and borders. Note: Styles selected as **Paragraph** style type will apply to the entire paragraph, even if only a few words of text are selected.
   - **Character** style will apply formatting characteristics only to text. Common characteristics include font name, size, color, bold, italic, underline, borders, and shading. Styles selected as **Character** type will apply only to the text that has been selected.
   - **Linked** style will behave either as a character style or a paragraph style, depending on what you have selected. If you click in a paragraph or select a complete paragraph, your style will be applied as a paragraph style. However, if you select only a single word or phrase within the paragraph, the style is applied as a character style and the rest of your paragraph will not be affected as a whole.

7. Click the **Style for following paragraph** dropdown arrow and click the name of the style you want to apply after a paragraph with the new style.

8. In the **Formatting** section, select the formatting options you want.

9. To have the style available from the **Quick Style Gallery**, select the **Add to Quick Style** list check box . If you want all new documents to be based on this custom style you have created, click the **New documents based on this template** radio button .

10. Click **OK** . Note: **Quick Styles** will only apply to the document you are working in. To save your custom **Quick Style** for use in other documents, save your document as a **Quick Style Set**.

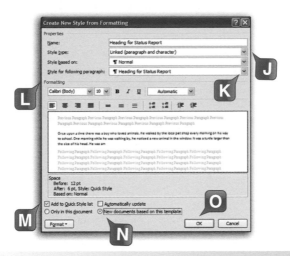

 Quickest Click: To save a style to the **Quick Style** gallery, highlight the text with the format you want to save, then right-click. Click **Styles**, then select **Save Selection as a New Quick Style** P from the fly out menu to open the **Create New Style from Formatting** dialog box.

 Hot Tip: You can save your style set as the default style for all new documents by clicking **Set as Default** Q under the **Change Styles** dropdown menu in the Styles group.

15 Apply a Consistent Look and Feel to a Document

Difficulty: ●●○○

PROBLEM You are satisfied with the content of your document, but you want to apply a coordinated color palette to create a professional and polished finish.

SOLUTION Apply a **Theme**. **Themes** are made up of colors, fonts, graphics, and effects that help you add a coordinated element of design to your documents. You can quickly format an entire document (or even a set of documents) by applying a theme. Microsoft Word 2010 comes with a variety of predesigned **Themes** to choose from.

See Also: Create a Custom Theme

Step-by-Step

View and Apply a Theme

1. Open the document you want to edit.

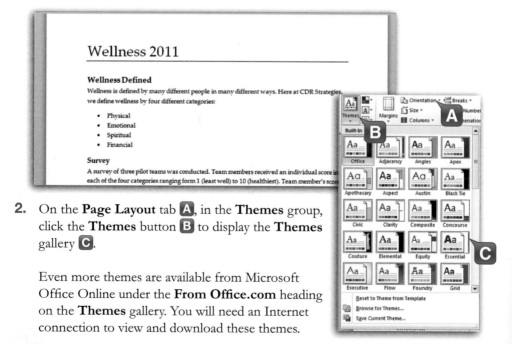

2. On the **Page Layout** tab **A**, in the **Themes** group, click the **Themes** button **B** to display the **Themes** gallery **C**.

   Even more themes are available from Microsoft Office Online under the **From Office.com** heading on the **Themes** gallery. You will need an Internet connection to view and download these themes.

3. Hover your cursor over a theme. Your document will change, providing a preview of that theme.

4. Click the theme you want to apply.

 Bright Idea: Microsoft Office's themes are available to all Office programs. Create consistent, polished, and professional looking presentations by using the same theme for your Excel, PowerPoint and Word documents.

16 Create a Custom Theme

Difficulty: ●●○○

PROBLEM Your marketing team has launched a new branding campaign for your organization. All of the colors, images, and fonts have changed to project a more modern image. You must create a new look and feel for all documentation to match the new branding scheme.

SOLUTION Create a custom theme. Using a pre-set theme is fast and easy, but a custom theme provides some additional benefits. A custom theme allows you to incorporate your organization's colors, fonts, graphics, and style into your document's appearance. You can either create a theme from scratch, or you can modify an existing theme.

See Also: Apply a Consistent Look and Feel to a Document

 What Microsoft Calls It: Theme or Document Theme

Step-by-Step

Create Theme Color Set

There are 12 page elements, including text/ background, accent, and hyperlinks, which may have colors assigned to them. Each element must be assigned a color.

1. On the **Page Layout** tab **A**, in the **Themes** group **B**, open the theme **Colors** menu **C**.

2. Choose **Create New Theme Colors** **D** to open the **Create New Theme Colors** dialog box.

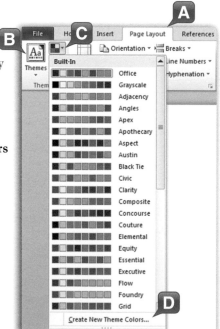

3. Click one of the colors **E**, or select **More Colors** **F** to launch the **Colors** dialog box **G** to select an alternate color.

4. Repeat this step for all elements **H**.

5. In the **Name** box **I**, type a name for the color scheme.

6. Click **Save** **J** to create new color set.

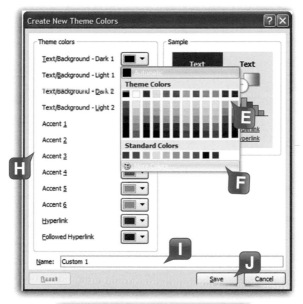

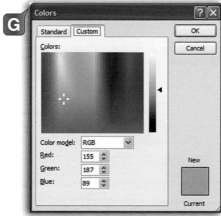

Step-by-Step

Create Theme Font Set

1. On the **Page Layout** tab, in the **Theme** group, click the **Fonts** button **K**.

2. Select **Create New Theme Fonts L** to launch the **Create New Theme Fonts** dialog box.

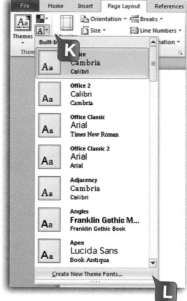

3. Use the dropdown menus to select **Heading** and **Body** fonts **M**.

4. In the **Name** box **N**, type a name for the new font set.

5 Click **Save O** to create new font set.

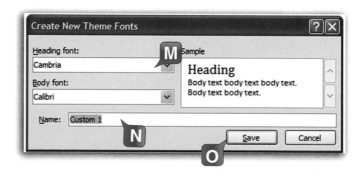

Step-by-Step

Choose and Apply a Custom Theme

1. On the **Page Layout** tab, in the **Themes** group, click the **Themes** button **P**.

2. Click **Browse for Themes Q**.

3. If you want to open a specific file type, click the **Files of Type** drop-down arrow **R**, and then select the **Office Theme** file type.

4. If your file is located in another folder, browse to locate the folder.

5. Click the theme file you want, and then click **Open S**.

17 | Apply a Watermark to a Page

Difficulty: ●○○○

PROBLEM You create a draft of a document and want to send it out for review. However, you want to make it clear to readers that this is a draft and not a final version.

SOLUTION A watermark is text that appears behind the main body of a document in the form of a grayed-out image. In Microsoft Word 2010, you can select from several pre-set watermarks or create a watermark using custom text. Watermarks are typically used to mark documents as CONFIDENTIAL or DRAFT. However, watermarks can consist of symbols (© ™ ®), company names, or even images.

Step-by-Step

---

Add a Watermark

1. On the **Page Layout** tab, in the **Page Background** group, click the **Watermark** button **A**.

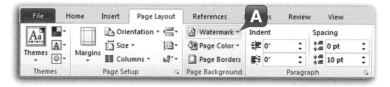

2. Select a watermark.

   a. In the menu, scroll down to select a pre-formatted watermark **B**.

   b. Create a custom watermark, by clicking **Custom Watermark C** from the **Watermark** dropdown menu to launch the **Printed Watermark** dialog box **D**. Select the radio button beside the type of watermark you want:

- **E** **No watermark:** When this option is selected, no watermark will appear in the document. Choose this if you wish to remove any existing watermark images or text , or click the **Remove watermark** option from the **Watermark** dropdown menu **F**.

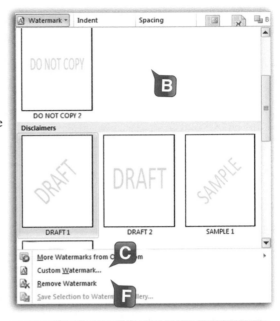

CONTINUE

- **Picture watermark G**: This option places a picture behind the main document in a washed-out format so it doesn't obstruct the main text of the document.

- Click the **Select Picture H** button to launch the **Insert Picture I** dialog box. Browse to the location of the picture and select the image you want.

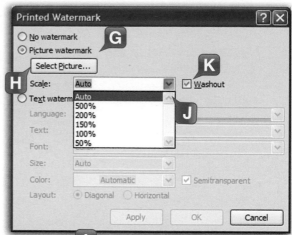

- Adjust the size of the image by choosing an option from the **Scale** dropdown menu **J**.

- If you do not want the picture washed-out, uncheck the **Washout** check box **K**.

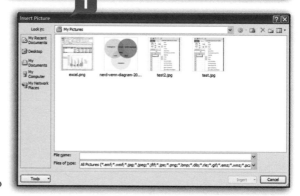

- **Text watermark L**: This option allows you to enter your own text as a watermark.

- Type your text into the **Text** text box **M**.

- Adjust the language, text, font, size, color, and layout of your text from the menu options.

- If you do not want the text semitransparent, uncheck the **Semitransparent** check box **N**.

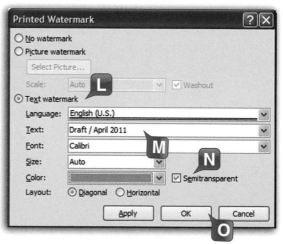

5. Click **OK O** to apply changes and return to document.

Course Objectives

Upon completion of the course, the student will be able to:

- Identify and accurately summarize the elements of an essay
  - Thesis
  - Main idea(s)
  - Supporting details
- Develop and support a thesis for different purposes and readers
- Employ the writing process
  - Invention
  - Planning
  - Drafting
  - Revision
- Demonstrate expressive, expository, and persuasive writing techniques using the principles of organization, unity, coherence, and theme development.
- Use documentation principles in a piece of writing
- Demonstrate critical thinking skills
- Differentiate between personal opinions and fact
- Use outside sources to synthesize ideas from multiple perspectives
- Draw informed conclusions from writings and observations
- Argue reasoned interpretations
- Critique one's own writing and the writings of others

Required Materials & REcommended Resources

Anderson, Gloria. *Writing for Excellence: Excellent Essays.* San Francisco: Scholastic, 2010.

Bastin, Warren. W. *Achieving Educational Excellence.* Boston: Jerry-Cross, 1995.

Burns, Laurel J. "A History of Writing Techniques." *Literature History.* URL: http://www.ccs.azu.edu/home/pb/lit-history.html (5 Dec. 2004).

Christie, Samantha S. "Words and Meaning: Grace Martinez's *Chronicle of a Story Well Told.*" *American Literary Review* 13.3 (Fall 2000): 21-29.

Evans, Charles. "The Decade of the Literary Essay: The 1890s." *Literature Division Lecture Series.* County Community College, Atlanta, 12 Sept 1999.

STOP

18

Add Information to the Tops or Bottoms of Pages

Difficulty: ●●●○

PROBLEM You produce identical reports on a regular basis, reflecting the most current status updates and memos. You need a way to keep track, at a glance, which version of a report you are looking at. You also want a way for the printed reports to stay organized so you can refer to page numbers during meetings.

SOLUTION Insert a **Header** and **Footer**. Headers and footers provide an excellent means of tracking version data, including revision dates and author changes. They can also make deciphering report information easier through the inclusion of navigation aids like page numbers, footnotes, and legends..

What Microsoft Calls It: Insert a header and footer

Step-by-Step

Insert and Configure Headers and Footers

1. Click the **Header** A or **Footer** B button in the **Header & Footer** group of the **Insert** tab.

2. Select from the dropdown **Header** or **Footer Gallery** C to add the header or footer template to your document D and activate the **Header & Footer** contextual tab E. ⚠

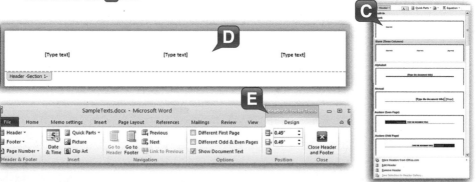

3. Type your information into the header/footer template as prompted. Replace temporary text **F** with your own **G**.

4. To insert and configure the elements you want displayed in your header or footer, place your cursor where you want a field to be placed, then click on the **QuickParts** button **H** on the **Insert** group of the contextual **Header & Footer Tools** tab.

5. Select the **Field** menu option **I** to open the **Field** dialog box.

6. In the **Field Names** box **J** in the **Please choose a field** panel of the Field dialog box, choose the field that you want to add to your header/footer. Some common field choices include:

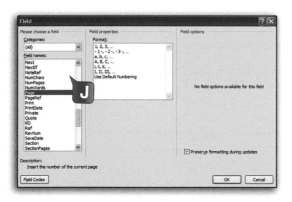

- **Page:** Displays the page number of the page that the **Page** field is located on.
- **NumPages:** Inserts the total number of pages in the document.
- **Date:** Inserts the current date .
- **CreateDate:** Inserts the date and time that a document was first saved with its current name, as recorded on the **Statistics** tab in the **Properties** dialog box.
- **SaveDate:** Inserts the date and time a document was last saved, using information ("Modified") on the **Statistics** tab in the **Properties** dialog box.
- **Time:** Inserts the current time.
- **FileName:** Inserts the full file name.
- **IncludePicture:** Inserts a picture.
- **Author:** Inserts the author name from the **Summary** tab in the **Properties** dialog box. To view the **Properties** dialog box, click the **File** tab, click **Info**, and click **Properties** (below the document preview on the right side), and then click **Advanced Properties**.
- **UserName:** Inserts the user name from the **User name** box in the **Word Options** dialog box. The **User name** box is located under **Personalize your copy of Microsoft Office** in the **Word Options** dialog box.
- **Bibliography:** Inserts the list of sources that are associated with your document, in alphabetical order, and in the style that you specified in the **Style** box of the **Citations & Bibliography** group on the **References** tab.

7. Choose any specific settings required for each field in the **Format** box under the **Field properties** panel **L** and **Field options** **M** panel.

8. Click **OK** to insert your field into the header/footer.

9. Choose your settings for how your headers/footers are going to display and print in the **Options** group **N**.

- **Different First Page:** Allows you to make a different header or footer (or no header and footer) on the first page of your document or section. This is very useful if the first page is a title page or if you want page numbers to begin on the second page of the document (as in many printed documents).

- **Different Odd & Even Pages:** Allows you to make different headers or footers depending on whether the page number is even or odd. Used most commonly in documents that will be printed book style where page numbers appear on the outside edges of the binding.

10. When your header or footer is complete, click the **Close Header and Footer** button  in the **Design** tab on the **Header & Footer Tools** contextual tab. If you need to make changes later, click on **Header** or **Footer** in the **Header & Footer** group on the **Insert** tab and select **Edit Header** from the dropdown gallery menu.

Caution: If you already have fields and text entered into a header or footer, choosing a new header or footer from the gallery will overwrite your existing content.

Bright Idea: If the document includes section breaks, each section can contain its own custom header and footer.

Quickest Click: To add only page numbers to a document, click the **Page Number** button from the **Header & Footer** group on the **Insert** tab. Select a page number placement and Style from the Gallery **R**. See caution above.

Quickest Click: To add or edit a header or footer, double click in the margins at the top or bottom of a page in the **Print Layout** view. This will open the header or footer editor view and activate the **Header & Footer Tools** tab.

19 | Insert and Customize WordArt

Difficulty: ●○○○

PROBLEM You are creating a yard sale flyer to send out to your neighborhood. You want the words "Yard Sale" to have an artistic look and draw attention.

SOLUTION **WordArt** is an object that combines graphic elements with text. **WordArt** is useful when you need to create quick and artistic ways of displaying company names, headings, graphics for flyers, or newsletter headings.

Step-by-Step

Creating WordArt Text

1. Place your cursor in your document where you want the **WordArt** to appear.

2. On the **Insert** tab in the **Text** group, click the **WordArt** button **A** and click one of the **WordArt** styles **B** to create a WordArt text box **C**.

3. In the **WordArt** text box, type the text you want **D**.

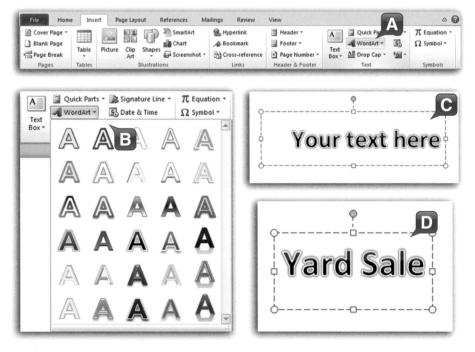

 Step-by-Step

Formating WordArt Text

1. Double-click the **WordArt** object you want to edit to activate the text box.

2. Click the **Format** tab **F** under the **Drawing Tools** contextual tab.

3. To change the shape style, select a new style from the **Shape Styles** gallery **G** in the **Shape Styles** group, or click the **More** arrow **H** to expand the selection **I**. Your document will preview the changes before you make your choice **J**.

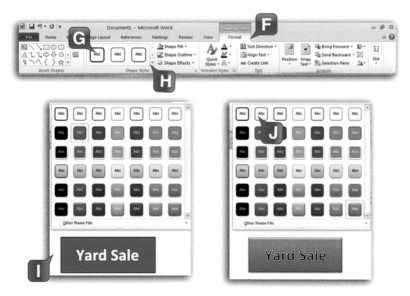

4. Click the **Style** you want to apply the changes.

5. To change the **Style, Fill, Outline** or **Text** effects of the **WordArt** text, use the options in the **WordArt Styles** group **K** in the **Format** tab under the **Drawing Tools** contextual tab. Select the text you want to change, but preview the changes **L** before you make your choice **M**.

6. Click the style you want to apply the changes.

7. To change to a completely different **WordArt Quick Style**, click the **Quick Styles** button **N** in the **WordArt Styles** group and choose a new **Quick Style**.

Hot Tip: You can convert text in an existing text box into **WordArt**. Select the text box, then click the **Insert** tab. Click the **WordArt** button, then click the WordArt style that you'd like to apply.

20 | Insert a Picture or Piece of Clip Art

Difficulty: ●○○○

PROBLEM You want to place images into your document that will enhance the content and presentation of your Word project.

SOLUTION Graphics are used to enhance design and to support text in documents. Graphics can be pasted or inserted, with the latter being preferred. You may insert graphics from your computer files, disks, or other storage devices, or you may select illustrations, borders, photos or backgrounds from the Microsoft **Clip Art Gallery**.

See Also: Arrange Images Around Text, Edit an Image's Colors and Stack Images and Group Images in a Document

 Step-by-Step

---

Insert an Image

1. Position the cursor where the image should be placed.

2. On the **Insert** tab, in the **Illustrations** group, select the **Picture** button **A**.

3. In the **Picture** dialog box **B**, browse to select the location of your image, select it, and click **Insert** **C** to place it in the document.

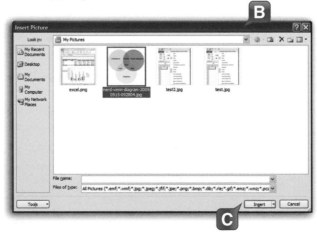

 **Step-by-Step**

Insert Clip Art

1. Position the cursor where the **Clip Art** should be placed.

2. On the **Insert** tab, in the **Illustrations** group, select the **Clip Art** button **D** to launch the **Clip Art** task pane.

3. In the **Search for** text box **E**, type a keyword to find the kind of picture you are looking for.

4. Click the **Go** button **F** to search for clip art that matches your keyword.

5. Click an image to insert it into your document.

6. Click the **Close** button **G** on the task pane when you are finished inserting clip art.

CONTINUE

Hot Tip: For more **Clip Art** selections, click the **Include Office.com content** checkbox 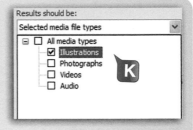 H to gain access to all the Clip Art available on Office.com. You will need an Internet connection for this to work. Clicking on the **Find more at Office.com** link I at the bottom of the **Clip Art** task pane will open a browser window to Microsoft's complete online collection of art.

Bright Idea: Narrow your selection by using the **Results should be** dropdown J in the **Clip Art** task pane. By checking only **Illustrations** K for example, you will only have to browse through art that is hand drawn and more casual. If your document requires more formal or realistic images, click the **Photographs** option to view only photographic images.

Results should be:

Selected media file types

- ☐ All media types
  - ☑ Illustrations
  - ☐ Photographs
  - ☐ Videos
  - ☐ Audio

Bright Idea: Shrink your document's file size by compressing images and removing cropped area data. To compress images in your document, select any image and then click the **Compress Pictures** button in the **Adjust** group on the **Format** tab. You may apply compression to just the selected image or to all images in the document.

21 | Arrange Images Around Text

Difficulty: ●●○○

PROBLEM The image you have inserted into your document is pushing text around the page in a disruptive way.

SOLUTION Edit the image and adjust the text wrapping settings to create the page layout you want.

The text wrapping style of an image or object determines how it interacts with text on the page. By specifying whether your image appears behind or in front of text, and how the text flows around your image, you can control not only how the image will appear on the page, but how it will act when text is added or deleted. Cropping, resizing, and rotating are useful tools for adjusting the image itself.

Step-by-Step

---

Adjust Text Wrapping

1. Click on the image you want to adjust. The **Picture Tools** contextual tab **A** will appear. Click the **Format** tab **B**.

2. Click the **Wrap Text** button **C** in the **Arrange** group.

3. Select the Wrapping Style you want **D** from the **Wrap Text** dropdown:

- **In Line with Text**

Baseball – The Great American Pastime

When attending a baseball game, it's important to remember why people are there. First, there's the game itself – the balls, the bats, the diamond, the dirt, RBIs and home runs. These things are idols to a true baseball fan. Second, there's the experience – the smell of fresh cooked hotdogs and fresh mown grass, the yelling (and even the vulgarity – it happens. You know who you are.) Lastly, there's the food! Beer, peanuts, crackerjacks and brats taste better when eaten while sitting in a hard plastic chair and cheering for your home team.

The earliest known reference to baseball is in a 1744 British publication, A Little Pretty Pocket-Book, by John Newbery. It contains a rhymed description of "base-ball" and a woodcut that

- **Square**

Baseball – The Great American Pastime

When attending a baseball game, it's important to remember why people are there. First, there's the game itself – the balls, the bats, the diamond, the dirt, RBIs and home runs. These things are idols to a true baseball fan. Second, there's the experience – the smell of fresh cooked hotdogs and fresh mown grass, the yelling (and even the vulgarity – it happens. You know who you are.) Lastly, there's the food! Beer, peanuts, crackerjacks and brats taste better when eaten while sitting in a hard plastic chair and cheering for your home team.

The earliest known reference to baseball is in a 1744 British publication, A Little Pretty Pocket-Book, by John Newbery. It contains a rhymed description of "base-ball" and a woodcut that shows a field set up somewhat similar to the modern game—though in a triangular rather than diamond configuration, and with posts instead of ground-level bases [5] English lawyer William Bray recorded a game of baseball on Easter Monday 1755 in Guildford, Surrey; Bray's diary was verified as authentic September 2008. [6] This early form of the game was apparently brought to North America by English immigrants. Rounders was also brought tot he continent by both British and Irish immigrants. The first known American reference to baseball appears in a

- **Tight**

Baseball – The Great American Pastime

When attending a baseball game, it's important to remember why people are there. First, there's the game itself – the balls, the bats, the diamond, the dirt, RBIs and home runs. These things are idols to a true baseball fan. Second, there's the experience – the smell of fresh cooked hotdogs and fresh mown grass, the yelling (and even the vulgarity – it happens. You know who you are.) Lastly, there's the food! Beer, peanuts, crackerjacks and brats taste better when eaten while sitting in a hard plastic chair and cheering for your home team.

The earliest known reference to baseball is in a 1744 British publication, A Little Pretty Pocket-Book, by John Newbery. It contains a rhymed description of "base-ball" and a woodcut that shows a field set up somewhat similar to the modern game—though in a triangular rather than diamond configuration, and with posts instead of ground-level bases [5] English lawyer William Bray recorded a game of baseball on Easter Monday 1755 in Guildford, Surrey; Bray's diary was verified as authentic September 2008. [6] This early form of the game was apparently brought to North America by English immigrants. Rounders was also brought tot he continent by both British and

- **Behind Text**

> **Baseball – The Great American Pastime**
>
> When attending a baseball game, it's important to remember why people are there. First, there's the game itself – the balls, the bats, the diamond, the dirt, RBIs and home runs. These things are idols to a true baseball fan. Second, there's the experience – the smell of fresh cooked hotdogs and fresh mown grass, the yelling (and even the vulgarity – it happens. You know who you are.) Lastly, there's the food! Beer, peanuts, crackerjacks and brats taste better when eaten while sitting in a hard plastic chair and cheering for your home team.
>
> The earliest known reference to baseball is in a 1744 British publication, A Little Pretty Pocket-book, by John Newbery. It contains a rhymed description of "base-ball" and a woodcut that shows a field that similar to the modern game—though in a triangular rather than diamond configuration, and with posts instead of ground-level bases [5] English lawyer William Bray recorded a game of baseball on Easter Monday 1755 in Guildford, Surrey; Bray's diary was verified as authentic in September 2008. [6] This early form of the game was apparently brought to North America by English immigrants. Rounders was also brought tot he continent by both British and Irish immigrants. The first known American reference to baseball appears in a 17092 Pittsfield, Massachusetts, town bylaw prohibiting the playing of the game near the town's new meeting house. [7] By 1796, a version of the game was well-known enough to earn a mention in a German scholar's book on popular pastimes. As described by Johann Gutsmuths, "englische

- **In Front of Text**

> **Baseball – The Great American Pastime**
>
> When attending a baseball game, it's important to remember why people are there. First, there's the game itself – the balls, the bats, the diamond, the dirt, RBIs and home runs. These things are idols to a true baseball fan. Second, there's the experience – the smell of fresh cooked hotdogs yelling (and even the vulgarity – it happens. You know who you are.) eer, peanuts, crackerjacks and brats taste better when eaten while air and cheering for your home team.
>
> nce to baseball is in a 1744 British publication, A Little Pretty Pocket-It contains a rhymed description of "base-ball" and a woodcut that hat similar to the modern game—though in a triangular rather than d with posts instead of ground-level bases [5] English lawyer William aseball on Easter Monday 1755 in Guildford, Surrey; Bray's diary was mber 2008. [6] This early form of the game was apparently brought to North America by English immigrants. Rounders was also brought tot he continent by both British and Irish immigrants. The first known American reference to baseball appears in a 17092 Pittsfield, Massachusetts, town bylaw prohibiting the playing of the game near the town's new meeting house. [7] By 1796, a version of the game was well-known enough to earn a mention in a German scholar's book on popular pastimes. As described by Johann Gutsmuths, "englische

- **Top and Bottom**

> **Baseball – The Great American Pastime**
>
> When attending a baseball game, it's important to remember why people are there. First, there's the game itself – the balls, the bats, the diamond, the dirt, RBIs and home runs. These things are idols to a true baseball fan. Second, there's the experience – the smell of fresh cooked hotdogs
>
>
>
> and fresh mown grass, the yelling (and even the vulgarity – it happens. You know who you are.) Lastly, there's the food! Beer, peanuts, crackerjacks and brats taste better when eaten while sitting in a hard plastic chair and cheering for your home team.

- **Through**

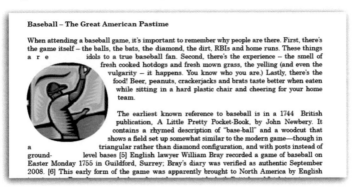

Step-by-Step

Crop, Resize, or Rotate an Image

1. Click on the image you want to adjust. **The Picture Tools** contextual tab **A** will appear. Click the **Format** tab **B**.

   - To resize the image, either click the up or down arrows in the **Shape Height E** or **Shape Width F** boxes in the **Size** group or type in the specific measurements you want. By default, the **aspect ratio** will be locked, and the shape will expand or shrink in proportion to its original size.

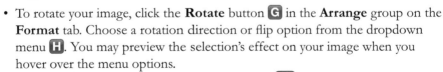

   - To rotate your image, click the **Rotate** button **G** in the **Arrange** group on the **Format** tab. Choose a rotation direction or flip option from the dropdown menu **H**. You may preview the selection's effect on your image when you hover over the menu options.

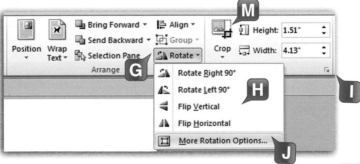

CONTINUE

- For more resizing and rotation options, click on the **Advanced Layout: Size** dialog box launcher on the **Size** group **I** or the **More Rotation Options...** **J** menu item in the **Rotate** dropdown menu.

  On the **Size** tab **K** in the **Layout** dialog box, adjust your image's size or rotation. This is also where you can unlock the aspect ratio and adjust size by percentage. Click **OK** **L** to apply your changes.

- To crop the image, click the **Crop** button **M** in the **Size** group on the **Format** tab. Black line **handles** **N** will be added to the image. Click and drag the handles to trim unneeded edges of your image. When you click away from the image, the cropped sections will disappear. Click **Crop** again to see the complete image.

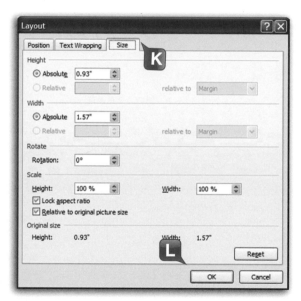

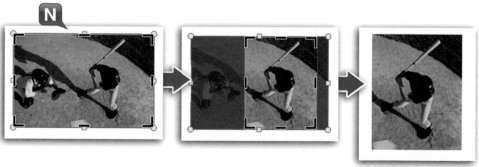

 Quickest Click: You can resize and rotate a shape manually by clicking and dragging any of the **size handles**  that appear when an object is selected. Clicking and dragging the green handle **P** allows you to rotate the image.

 Quickest Click: Many of the above features are available at a click. Click on your image, then right-click. To change wrapping style, click **Wrap Text** to see style options. **Crop, Rotate, Height** and **Width** menus are also available in the right-click pop-up.

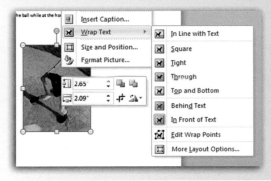

 Hot Tip: Keep in mind the importance of design principles when including graphic elements into documents. A picture should add to, not detract from, the message. Principles of balance, symmetry, and color, for example, should also be considered.

22 Edit an Image's Colors

Difficulty: ●○○○

PROBLEM You want to put an image of a house into your document to support the content. You have a great image, but the color clashes with the rest of the images in the document.

SOLUTION Word 2010 includes several robust image editing tools, including those that allow you to make changes to an image's color, transparency, brightness, contrast and more. Graphics are used to enhance the design and to support the text in documents. Once a graphic is placed into a document, it can be formatted so that it fits with your text and other document elements.

See Also: Insert a Picture or Clip Art; Stack and Group Images in a Document

Step-by-Step

Adjust Image Color

1. Click on the image you want to adjust. The **Picture Tools** contextual tab **A** will appear. Click the **Format** tab **B**.

2. In the **Adjust** group, select the **Color** button **C**. If the graphic is a photograph, the **Color** dropdown menu will allow you to edit **Color Saturation, Color Tone**, and give you **Recolor** options. If the graphic is an illustration, you will only see the **Recolor** options.

   The image's current settings will be highlighted **D**. Preview the selections by hovering over the options.

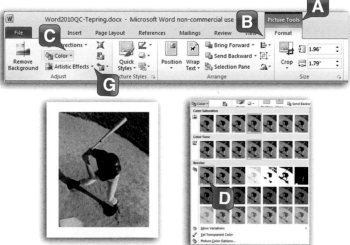

- **Color Saturation:** Saturation describes the intensity of the color in a photograph. A higher saturation will make a picture look more vivid, the colors more bright. A lower saturation shades the colors towards gray.

- **Color Tone:** Color tone describes the dominant color influencing a picture. When a camera does not measure the color temperature correctly, for example, a picture can look too blue or too orange. The Color Tone allows you to adjust the color temperature to enhance picture details and make the picture look better. The higher the temperature, the more orange is added to your picture. The lower the temperature, the more blue is added.

- **Recolor:** Recolor gives you a set of built-in stylized effects. Some options like grayscale or sepia are common color changes. You can also choose to recolor your image based upon your document's Theme, allowing you to match images or illustrations to your theme's color palette for a professional and consistent look.

CONTINUE

Step-by-Step

Set Transparent Color

You may want to make part of your picture transparent to make it work better with text that is layered on top or beneath it. Transparent areas in a picture appear as the same color as the paper on which it is printed or the background on which it is displayed (as on a Website). Only one color per picture can be set to transparent in Word 2010.

1. Click on the image you want to adjust. The **Picture Tools** contextual tab **A** will appear. Click the **Format** tab **B**.

2. In the **Adjust** group, select the **Color** button **C** to open the **Picture Color** dropdown menu. Click **Set Transparent Color** menu option **E**.

3. Your curser will turn to a color selection tool **F**. Click the color in the picture or illustration that you want to make transparent. ⚠

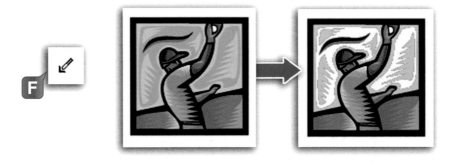

Caution: If the picture you are using has a lot of variation of color (such as a photograph of the sunset), this option will not be as useful. The transparency tool is most useful in an image with solid color backgrounds.

Hot Tip: For even more artistic options, click on the **Artistic Effects** button G in the **Adjust** group of the **Format** tab. From here, you can choose effects like **Pencil Sketch, Cement**, and **Glow Edges** that will change your photograph's look and design.

23 | Add Style to Images

Difficulty: ●○○○

PROBLEM You have graphics in your document that enhance your message, but you want them to stand out from the surrounding text. You want them to pop off the page and have a designer look.

SOLUTION Add style to your images with borders and effects. Word 2010 includes many style options to enhance and spice up your images. Borders and frames can set your graphics apart from the surrounding text. 3D effects, shadows, reflections, and blur can give your visual objects a custom look.

Step-by-Step

Add a Quick Style

1. Click on the image you want to adjust. The **Picture Tools** contextual tab  will appear. Click the **Format** tab **B**.

2. In the **Picture Styles** group, select the **More** button **C** in the **Quick Styles** selection box to open the **Quick Styles** dropdown **D**.

3. Choose from the border and effects combinations. Preview the selections by hovering over the choices.

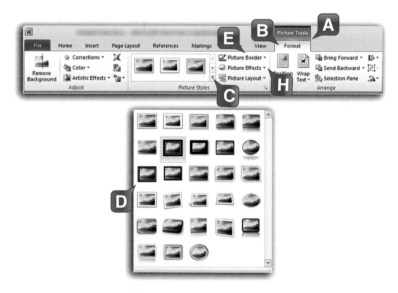

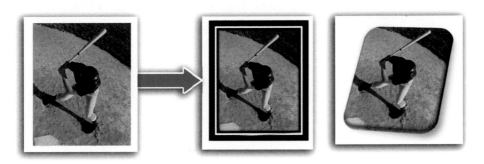

Step-by-Step

Create Your Own Styles

1. Click on the image you want to enhance. The **Picture Tools** contextual tab **A** will appear. Click the **Format** tab **B**.

    - Add a border to your image: click the **Picture Border** button **E** in the **Picture Styles** group. Select a color for your border from the **Theme Color** palette **F**. Choose the thickness of your border from the **Line Weight** pop-out menu **G**. Preview your selections by hovering over the choices.

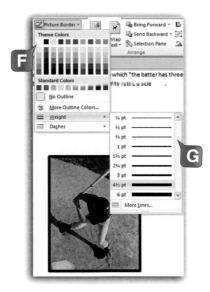

- Add an effect to your image: Click the **Picture Effects** button  in the **Picture Styles** group. Select an effect for your image from the Picture Effects dropdown menus . Preview your selections by hovering over the choices.

Hot Tip: For even more control over effects, click on the **Format Picture** dialog box launcher **J** or any **Options** link **K** to launch the **Format Picture** dialog box **L**.

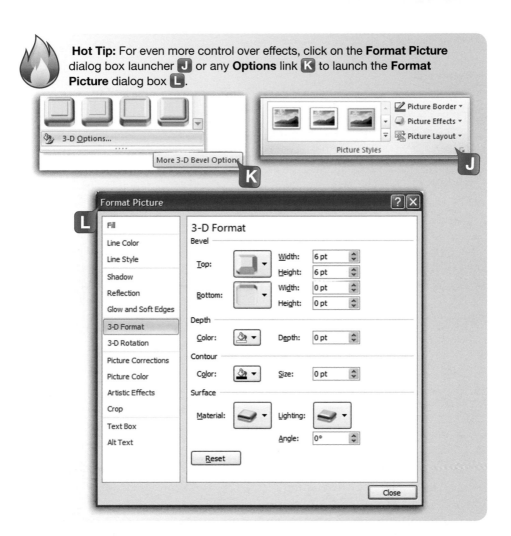

Caution: Print a test page to check the image quality in its final format to be certain your changes look as you expect. For example, if the edited image looks good in color, but will be printed in black and white, it should be reviewed before finalizing.

24 | Stack and Group Images in a Document

Difficulty: ●○○○

PROBLEM You want to create images that overlap one another.

SOLUTION Multiple objects in a document appear in a stacking order, like layers of transparent paper. Stacking is the placement of objects one on top of another. The first object that you draw is on the bottom, and the last object is on the top. You can change the order of these objects by using layering commands. When creating an object consisting of multiple individual shapes, editing those individually can be challenging. Objects can be grouped, ungrouped, or grouped again to make editing easier.

Stack objects on top of one another when you want to create overlapping shapes, add text to an image, or use arrows to point to specific areas in a graphic. You can also move graphics in front of or behind the text layer, like a Watermark, for example.

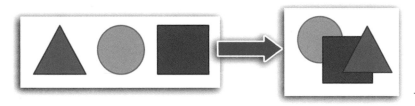

Step-by-Step

If you intend to layer items, you must first make sure that **In Line with Text** is not selected as the image's **Text Wrapping** option. To make sure any selection except **In Line with Text** is chosen, click the image to select it, and then click the **Wrap Text** button **A** in the **Arrange Group** on the **Format** tab. ✳

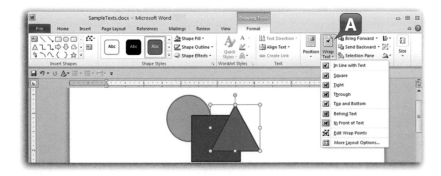

1. Select the object to layer.

2. On the **Page Layout** tab, in the **Arrange** group, click **Bring Forward** 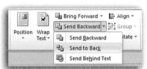 or **Send Backward**  to move an object up or down one position within the layers. By default, graphics are stacked in the order they are drawn.

3. To move an object all the way forward or all the way back, open the dropdown in the **Bring Forward** or **Send Backward** combo button .

4. Click either **Bring to Front** or **Send to Back**.

 **Step-by-Step**

Group Shapes

If you intend to group items, you must first make sure that **In Line with Text** is not selected as the image's text wrapping option. To make sure any selection except **In Line with Text** is chosen, click the image to select it, and then click the **Wrap Text** button **A** in the **Arrange** group on the **Format** tab.

1. Select the pieces to be grouped. ⚠
   • Click and drag a box around the entire collection.
   • Hold the CTRL key as you click each item to add it to the selection.

2. Click the **Format** tab **B** under the **Drawing** or **Picture Tools** contextual tab, depending on what type of object your image is.

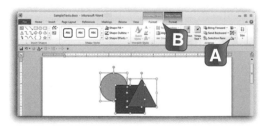
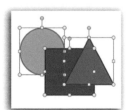

3. Click the **Group** button **C** in the **Arrange** group.

4. Click **Group**. Individual selection handles disappear and a single set of selection handles **D** appears for the whole group. ✳

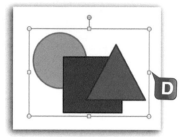

Step-by-Step

Ungroup Shapes

1. Select the grouped object you want to ungroup.

2. Click the **Format** tab **B** under **Drawing Tools** or **Picture Tools** contextual tabs.

3. Click the **Group** button **C** in the **Arrange** group.

4. Click **Ungroup** **E**. Individual selection handles return for each object.

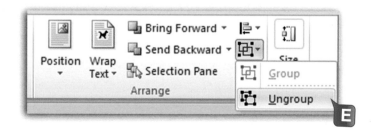

Quickest Click: To change the text wrapping, select your object then right-click. Select **Wrap Text** F from the fly out menu and make your text wrapping changes. You can also **Bring to Front** and **Send to Back** G from the right-click fly out menu.

Quickest Click: To group shapes, select all the objects you want grouped, then right-click. Select **Grouping** from the fly out menu and then **Group** H.

Caution: Some items will not easily group together. If you find your objects will not group, you need to place them on a **Drawing Canvas.** To create a **Drawing Canvas**, click the **Shapes** button I in the **Illustration** group on the **Insert** tab and select **New Drawing Canvas** J. This will insert a bordered frame. Cut and paste each item—one at a time—from its current location to the **Drawing Canvas**. Once the objects are on the canvas, you should be able to group them.

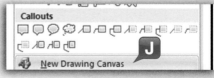

25 Create a List of All Illustrations in a Document

Difficulty: ●●○○

PROBLEM You created a technical product guide for one of your best-selling products. The product guide contains a large number of images, charts, and figures. Your customers have mentioned that it would help to have a way to quickly scan through the diagrams to find the one they are looking for, instead of flipping through pages.

SOLUTION Create a Table of Figures. A Table of Figures is similar to a Table of Contents, but it indexes diagrams and captions instead of headings. This is useful in documents like technical manuals or scientific reports that include a large number of figures or diagrams. The table can be positioned after the Table of Contents, allowing reviewers easy access to a list of illustrations.

See Also: Insert a Picture or Piece of Clip Art; Edit an Image's Colors

 **What Microsoft Calls It:** Insert a Table of Figures

Step-by-Step

Create Captions

Captions are helpful not only to connect images with your content, but also to provide more information about the illustration. Adding captions to images is also the first step in creating a Table of Figures.

1. Right-click on the graphic that needs a caption and select **Insert Caption A** to launch the **Caption** dialog box.

2. In the **Caption** text box **B**, type a descriptive caption. The numbering is pre-filled.

3. Select the position where you want the caption to appear, above or below, from the **Position** dropdown menu **C**.

4. Click **OK D** to apply the caption. An editable text box **E** will appear next to your image in the position you have chosen.

5. Repeat these steps for all the images you want in the **Table of Figures.**

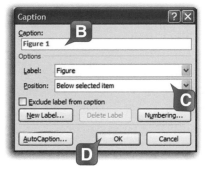

Step-by-Step

Create a Table of Figures

1. Place your cursor where you want to insert a **Table of Figures.**

2. On the **References** tab in the **Captions** group, click **Insert Table of Figures** **F** to launch the **Table of Figures** dialog box.

3. Select the tab leader (pattern of dots between the entry and the page number) you want to use from the **Tab Leader** dropdown list **G**. Your choice will be updated in the **Print Preview** pane **H**.

4. Select the format you want for the **Table of Figures** from the **Formats** dropdown list **I**.

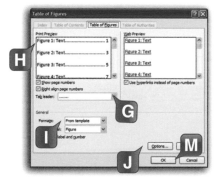

CONTINUE

5. Click on the **Options** button 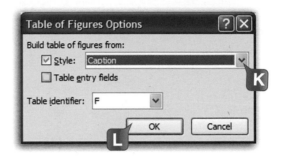 to open the **Table of Figures Options** dialog box.

6. Select **Caption** from the **Style** dropdown menu. Click **OK** to close the **Table of Figures Options**.

7. Click **OK** to insert **Table of Figures** into document.

Figure 1 2010 Batting Statistics *2*
Figure 2 Proper Batting Stance *2*
Figure 3 Baseball, America's Pastime *2*

Bright Idea: If your document will contain many graphs and imported objects (such as Excel Worksheets and PowerPoint slides) you can save time adding captions for a **Table of Figures** by using the **AutoCaption** feature. In the **Caption** dialog box, click the **Auto Caption** button to launch the **AutoCaption** dialog box **O**. Choose which objects will be included and set your **Use label** and **Position** preferences. Click **OK**.

26 | Insert Text Box

Difficulty: ●○○○

PROBLEM As an account manager for a small boutique, you have been asked to create a one-page flyer promoting a new product. Instead of spending the money to hire someone for such a simple project, you would like to do it yourself.

SOLUTION A text box is a shape designed to place text in a document without interacting with standard page margins. Text boxes are especially useful when adding text to a graphic image. However, text boxes are frequently used to enhance the design of professional documents.

Depending upon the application of a text box, you can either select one of the available presets, or design a custom text box by drawing and formatting the elements. Text can be added to virtually any shape inserted via the Shapes button in the Illustrations group on the Insert tab, whether they are specialized for that purpose (such as thought bubbles and call-outs) or basic figures like squares, cylinders and stars.

Step-by-Step

1. On the **Insert** tab in the **Text** group, click **Text Box A**.

2. Several standard text box samples are available to preview and select in the **Text Box** menu **B** or select the option to **Draw Text Box C**.

   - The standard options will place a text box template into the document. Replace default text with your own.

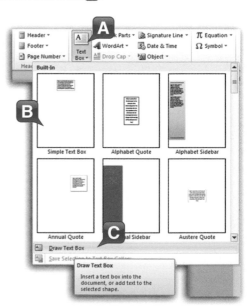

- Drawing a custom text box allows you to customize the formatting elements of the text box, such as size, font, colors, and borders and shading.

3. The text box may be moved anywhere in the document by clicking and dragging (or copying/cutting and pasting) it to the preferred location.

Step-by-Step

Format the Text Box

Place your cursor in the text box. The **Drawing Tools** contextual tab **D** appears on the main ribbon. By selecting the elements in the **Format** tab **E**, you can reformat the following elements of your text box:

- Text **F**
- Text Box Style **G**
- Shadow and 3-D Effects **H**

- Text Box Arrangement
- Size

Click Here for Results

CLICK HERE FOR RESULTS

CLICK HERE FOR RESULTS

Click Here for Results

Hot Tip: You can group text boxes and images together.

STOP

27 | Add a Table to a Document

Difficulty: ●●●○

PROBLEM You need to categorize the results from a recent wellness survey. You want to organize the data by team and topic.

SOLUTION Create a table to organize this data within the rest of your report. Tables are useful objects, consisting of columns and rows that help organize information in a logical, easy to view format. You can insert a preformatted table that includes sample data, or you can manually choose the number of rows and columns you need. Once created, you can adjust cells, insert or delete rows, columns, and cells, change the alignment of text, sort data, or apply borders and shading.

See Also: Format Table Layout; Format Table Text, Borders, and Shading; Import Data from an Excel Spreadsheet into a Document; Perform Calculations in a Table

Step-by-Step

Add a Table to a Document

1. Place the cursor where the table should be inserted into the document.
2. On the **Insert** tab, in the **Tables** group, click the **Table** button **A**.
3. Click **Insert Table B** to open the **Insert Table** dialog box.
4. Under **Table size**, enter the number of columns and rows **C** you need.

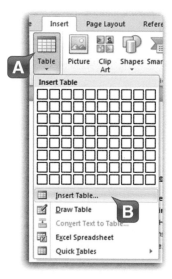

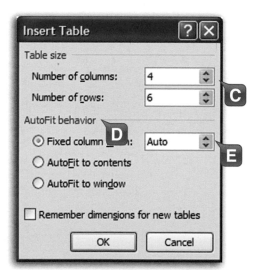

5. Under **AutoFit behavior** 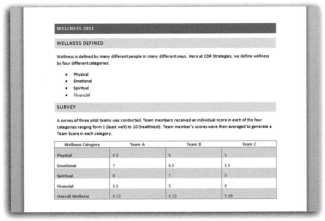, choose options to adjust the table size.

- **Fixed column width:** Auto setting will choose the best width for your page and fix the width to that setting. Click the **Up and Down** arrows **E** to set a fixed column width of your choosing in inches.

- **AutoFit to contents:** Columns will be set automatically based on the content that is included in the cells.

- **AutoFit to window:** Column size will be set according to the size of the window/page.

 Quickest Click: On the **Insert** tab, in the **Tables** group, click **Table** and drag the mouse to select the number of columns and rows for the table **F**. You can then format the size of the table by selecting the table in your document, then right clicking and selecting **Table Properties**.

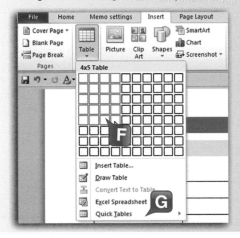

CONTINUE

Bright Idea: Word 2010 comes with several preformatted tables with common uses. Use a preformatted table to create a quick table by selecting the **Quick Tables** menu **G**, in the **Tables** dropdown menu on the **Insert** tab. Simply replace the data in the table with your information.

Hot Tip: You can convert text to a table with a few clicks by inserting separator characters, such as commas, to indicate where the text should separate into columns. Use paragraph marks to indicate a new row. Select the text to convert. On the **Insert** tab, in the **Tables** group, click the **Table** button. Click **Convert Text to Table.** In the box, click the option for the separator character that you used 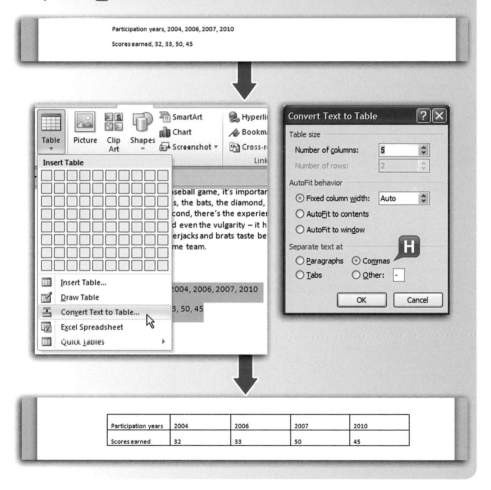 and click **OK**.

Participation years, 2004, 2006, 2007, 2010

Scores earned, 32, 33, 50, 45

Participation years	2004	2006	2007	2010
Scores earned	32	33	50	45

28 | Format Table Layout

Difficulty: ●●○○

PROBLEM You received updates to information that you already have incorporated into a table. You need to add columns and rows to accommodate the new data, and you would like a way to create a title row that spans several columns so the data is easier to read.

SOLUTION Once a generic table is built, there are a number of modifications that can be applied to the layout of that table. For example, you can add or delete rows and/or columns of the table. You can edit the size of the rows, columns, and cells, and can merge cells together or split one cell into multiple cells.

See Also: Add a Table to a Document

Step-by-Step

	Top Three Teams in the League		
	The Cougars	The Colts	The Chargers
Game 1	W	L	W
Game 2	W	W	L
Game 3	L	W	W
Game 4	L	W	L
Game 5	W	L	W
Game 6	W	W	W

Modify Row, Column, and Cell Height and Width

1. Select the portion of the table you want to modify.

2. Right-click anywhere in the table, then select **Table Properties** **A** from the menu to open the **Table Properties** dialog box.

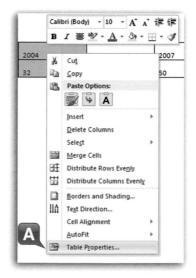

3. The **Table Properties** dialog box contains four tabs, each covering specific modifications, such as:

- **Table:** This tab allows you to modify the size (width) of table rows and columns, set the alignment and to define text wrapping preferences within the table.

- **Row:** This tab allows you to modify the size (height) of a row and define settings, such as whether to allow rows to break across pages, and if row information should be repeated at the top of each document page. This is typically done with a table that runs multiple pages and has a single header row at the top.

- **Column:** This tab allows you to modify the size (width) of a column.

- **Cell:** This tab allows you to modify the size of a specific cell, as well as its vertical alignment. If you have defined overall table size properties, you would only specify different information in this tab to create alternate formatting for a specific highlighted cell.

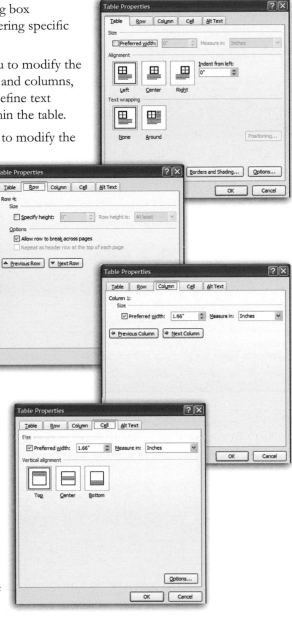

CONTINUE

Step-by-Step

Insert Rows or Columns

1. Place cursor in the position where a row or column should be added.

2. Right-click and select **Insert**  from the menu.

3. Select an option from the fly out menu C to set the place where the new column or row will go.

Step-by-Step

Merge Cells

1. Highlight the rows or columns to merge together.

2. Right-click and select **Merge Cells D**.

3. Note the changes to the way the text is presented **E**.

4. Edit text layout after merging cells to make sure it is formatted correctly.

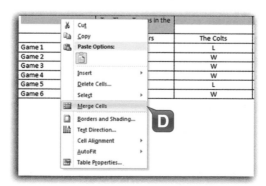

Top Three Teams in the League			
	The Cougars	The Colts	The Chargers
Game 1	W	L	W
Game 2	W	W	L
Game 3	L	W	W
Game 4	L	W	L
Game 5	W	L	W
Game 6	W	W	W

Step-by-Step

Split Cells

1. In the cells you wish to split into multiple columns or rows, right-click and select **Split Cells**  to open the **Split Cells** dialog box.

2. Set the number of rows and/or columns to split into.

3. Click **OK** to apply.

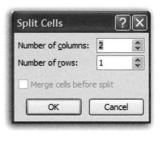

29 Format Table Text, Borders, and Shading

Difficulty: ●●○○

PROBLEM You have created a table and your data is correctly displayed in the columns and rows it needs. However, you would like to make the table look more attractive on the page and highlight every other row of your table to make the information even easier to read.

SOLUTION After you create a table, there are multiple options to format the table's borders, layout, and shading. These features enhance the table's design, usability, and function within the document.

Step-by-Step

Format Borders

In tables, "borders" are the lines surrounding cells. The borders in a table always exist—whether they are visible and printed or not. You can modify the visibility, style, color, and width of table borders.

1. Select the cell(s) you want to format.

2. On the **Design** tab  in the **Table Tools** contextual tab, click the **Borders** dropdown arrow **B**.

3. Select a border from the menu to either add or remove, or select **Borders and Shading C** to launch the **Borders and Shading** dialog box for custom formatting. ⚡

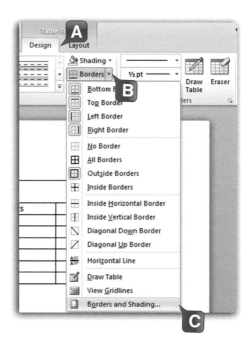

4. On the **Borders** tab of the **Borders and Shading** dialog box, select a border setting, style, color, and width for your borders.

5. Specify whether these settings should apply to the **Whole Table** or only to the selected cell(s) in the **Apply to** dropdown 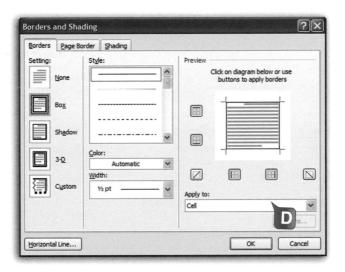.

   *Note: To remove all borders from the cell(s) or Table, click **None** under **Setting**.*

6. Click **OK** to accept the border settings.

Top Three Teams in the League			
	The Cougars	The Colts	The Chargers
Game 1	W	L	W
Game 2	W	W	L
Game 3	L	W	W
Game 4	L	W	L
Game 5	W	L	W
Game 6	W	W	W

Step-by-Step

Format Shading

Shading is a design element used to highlight or emphasize certain elements in the presentation of the data. To modify shading:

1. Select the cell(s) you want to format.

2. On the **Design** tab in the **Table Tools** contextual tab, click the **Shading** dropdown arrow 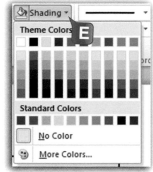.

3. Select a color from the menu to apply the color to the cells you have selected.

4. For more shading options, right-click on the selected cells in the table and select **Borders and Shading** from the menu to launch the **Borders and Shading** dialog box.

5. Click the **Shading** tab.

6. Select the fill color and/or patterns to shade the cell(s).

7. Specify whether these settings should apply to the whole table or to the selected cell(s) only in the **Apply to** dropdown menu.

8. Click **OK** to accept the shading settings.

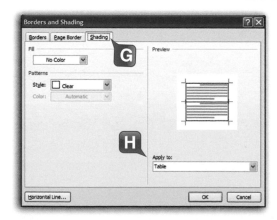

Top Three Teams in the League		
	The Cougars	The Colts	The Chargers
Game 1	W	L	W
Game 2	W	W	L
Game 3	L	W	W
Game 4	L	W	L
Game 5	W	L	W
Game 6	W	W	W

Format Text

The text within a table can be formatted like any other text in the document. Text elements such as alignment, size, style, font, and color can be modified.

1. Select the text to be formatted.

2. On the **Home** tab, in the **Font** group , edit the font, size, style, and color of the text by selecting the appropriate font edit tools.

3. On the **Home** tab, in the **Paragraph** group **J**, edit the font alignment and spacing by selecting the appropriate paragraph edit tools.

Top Three Teams in the League		
	The Cougars	The Colts	The Chargers
Game 1	W	L	W
Game 2	W	W	L
Game 3	L	W	W
Game 4	L	W	L
Game 5	W	L	W
Game 6	W	W	W

 Quickest Click: Right-click on the selected cells in the table and select **Borders and Shading** from the menu.

30 | Perform Calculations in a Table

Difficulty: ●●●○

PROBLEM You are working with a table of data in your Word project, and you want to insert calculations into the table to add or obtain an average of your numbers.

SOLUTION When using number data in a Word project, there is often a need to perform calculations. While you could perform these math functions on a calculator and simply type them in, this won't maintain accuracy if the figures ever change or if new figures are added.

See Also: Insert and Manage Stored Document Components; Add a Table to a Document; Format Table Text, Borders, and Shading; Format Table Layout; Create Templates

Step-by-Step

Calculate a Value in a Table

1. Place the cursor in the cell where the calculation will be performed.

2. Click the **Layout** tab under **Table Tools**.

3. Click the **Formula** button 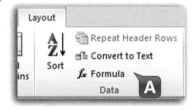 to open the **Formula** dialog box.

   Note: Word will auto-populate a formula **B** *based on common calculations that are used.*

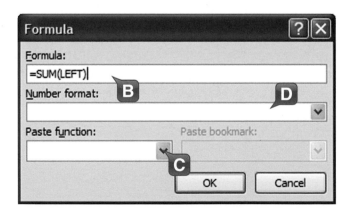

4. If the auto-populated format is not the one you need, click the **Paste Function** dropdown arrow **C** and select a function from the list.

5. To reference the contents of a table cell, type the cell name in the parentheses within the formula. For example, to average the values in cells a1 through a3, the formula would read **=Average(a1,a3)**.

6. In the **Number format** box **D**, select a format from the dropdown or enter a format for the numbers. For example, to display the numbers as a decimal percentage, select 0.00%. Enter 0 to display an average to the nearest whole number. To display a true average, enter 0.00 in the **Number Format** box.

7. Click **OK** to complete.

Bright Idea: If you are performing a simple operation, such as adding numbers of a column in the last row of the column, you can type **=Sum**. This will add together the numbers that appear in the column above the cell. If you are doing a similar operation in the last column of a row, you can type **=Sum (Left)**. This will add the numbers that appear in the row to the left of this cell.

Hot Tip: You can insert formulas anywhere in a document, not just in tables. You can also insert fields that update automatically each time you open the document. This can be handy for creating templates.

STOP

31 | Insert and Manage Stored Document Components

Difficulty: ●●●○

PROBLEM Your organization's senior members are required to submit reports on their segment of the association. It would be helpful if the reporting members had access to standardized document elements (such as headers, footers, and cover pages) to easily access and use.

SOLUTION A **Quick Part** is a defined field or set of fields you can pull into a document. Word calls these building blocks. Building blocks are elements within a document, or element templates that allow you to create standardized documents quickly and easily. These are different from traditional templates because they are document components, as opposed to complete documents. The components are contained in galleries and include such document elements as headers and footers, table of contents, cover pages, text boxes, watermarks, and even boilerplate text.

While Microsoft Word 2010 has default Building Block components available, you can create your own Building Blocks and save them in the Building Blocks gallery (Quick Parts) for use in future documents.

See Also: Perform Calculations in a Table; Create Templates; Insert Text Box

 What Microsoft Calls It: Building Blocks/Quick Parts

Step-by-Step

Creating a Building Block Component

1. Select the content you want to save as a building block, such as a custom header.

2. On the **Insert** tab, in the **Text** group, select **Quick Parts** dropdown button **A**.

3. Click **Save Selection to Quick Part Gallery** **B** from the **Quick Parts** dropdown to open the **Create New Building Block** dialog box.

4. Type a name for the **Quick Part** in the **Name** text box **C** and click **OK** **D**.

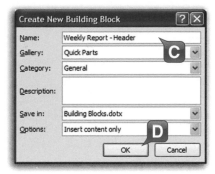

 Step-by-Step

Add a Custom Building Block Component to a Document

1. Open the document where the **Building block** component should appear.

2. Place the cursor where the **Building block** component will be inserted.

3. On the **Insert** tab, in the **Text** group, click the **Quick Parts** button **A**.

4. Saved **Building block** components will be listed along with a preview **E**.

5. Click on the **Building block** you want. It will be inserted into your document at the cursor.

Hot Tip: To view all available building blocks (system default and custom), click the **Building Blocks Organizer** in the **Quick Parts** menu.

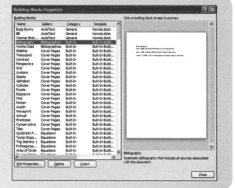

32 | Insert Manual Page Breaks

Difficulty: ●○○○

PROBLEM You are creating a long and complex document that includes pieces written by several different authors. You want each author's work to begin on a new page.

SOLUTION Insert a page break when you want to start a new page. This is useful when you want to separate content in your document. When you insert a page break, the text immediately after your page break will always appear on a new page.

Step-by-Step

1. Select the place in the document where the new page should begin **A**.

2. On the **Insert** tab in the **Pages** group, click **Page Break B**.

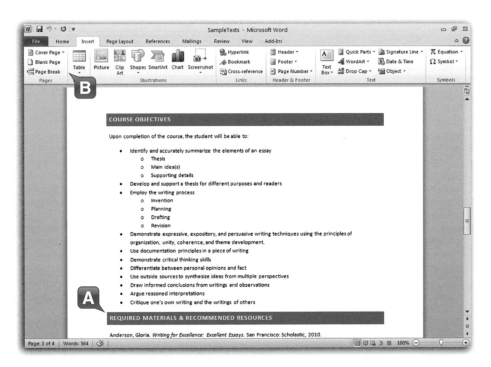

Original Page

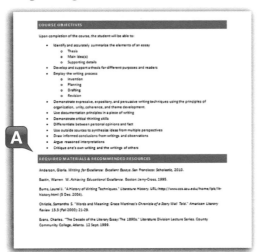

After Page Break

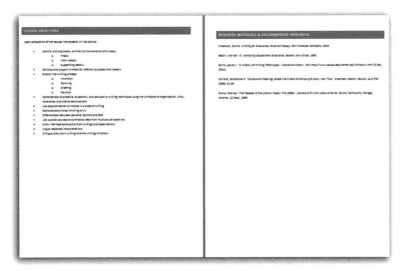

 Quickest Click: Place your cursor where you want to insert the page break and click **CTRL+Enter.**

33 | Divide Document into Sections

Difficulty: ●●○○

PROBLEM You have created a manual with several chapters, including an introduction. You want to begin page numbering after the introduction.

SOLUTION Section breaks divide your document into separate pieces, or sections. Each section can contain any number of pages and have its own formatting, including different headers and footers. The following elements can be edited separately for each section:

- Margins
- Paper size or orientation
- Paper source for a printer
- Page borders
- Alignment of text on a page
- Headers and footers
- Columns
- Page numbers
- Line numbers
- Footnotes and endnotes

See Also: Insert Text Box; Add Information to the Tops or Bottoms of Pages

 What Microsoft Calls It: Section Breaks

 **Step-by-Step**

1. Place your cursor at the position in the document where the section break should begin.

2. On the **Page Layout** tab, in the **Page Setup** group, click **Breaks** Ⓐ to open the dropdown menu.

3. Click the specific type of section break you want:

- **Next Page B**: Inserts a section break and starts the new section on the next page. This is useful for starting new chapters in a document.

- **Continuous C**: Inserts a section break and starts the new section on the same page. This is useful when creating a format change, such as utilizing different column layouts on a page.

- **Even Page D**: Inserts a section break and starts the new section on the next even numbered page. This is useful if you want chapters to always begin on an even page.

- **Odd Page E**: Inserts a section break and starts the new section on the next odd-numbered page. This is useful if you want chapters to always begin on an odd page, or if facing pages have different footers, such as page numbers in the outside margins.

Breaks ▾ | **Watermark ▾** | **Indent**

Page Breaks

Page
Mark the point at which one page ends and the next page begins.

Column
Indicate that the text following the column break will begin in the next column.

Text Wrapping
Separate text around objects on web pages, such as caption text from body text.

Section Breaks

Next Page
Insert a section break and start the new section on the next page.

Continuous
Insert a section break and start the new section on the same page.

Even Page
Insert a section break and start the new section on the next even-numbered page.

Odd Page
Insert a section break and start the new section on the next odd-numbered page.

Hot Tip: Turn on paragraph marks to see where section breaks are located. Click on the **Paragraph Marks** button ¶ in the **Paragraph** group on the **Home** tab.

Caution: Section breaks control the formatting of the text that precedes them. When you delete a section break, you also delete the section formatting for the text before the break. That text will become part of the following section and assume all formatting for that section. The break that controls the formatting for the last portion of your document is not displayed as part of the document. To change the document formatting, click in the last paragraph of the document.

34 | Insert a Hyperlink into a Document

Difficulty: ●○○○

PROBLEM Your Human Resources department creates and distributes a memo to employees regarding next year's benefit selections. There are several documents that need to be reviewed and some forms to be completed and returned by a certain date. Instead of sending these as attachments via e-mail, which will create a large file size and slow the process, you want to insert links to the additional files, along with instructions and a summary of each in the main document.

SOLUTION Insert hyperlinks to point to other files, web addresses, or locations within the same document. A hyperlink can be assigned to either text or graphics. When you click a hyperlink, the referenced "point to" location opens. These types of links are most often seen on web pages. However, they are frequently used in Word as a way to embed links to other files related to the main source document.

Step-by-Step

1. Select the text or the image that will be formatted as a hyperlink.

2. On the **Insert** tab in the **Links** group, click **Hyperlink** **A** to open the **Insert Hyperlink** dialog box. ⚡

3. Select the **Link to** hyperlink destination in the panel:
   - **Existing File or Web Page** **B**: Select this option if you want to link to another Word document on your computer or the network, or if you want to link to a web page.

     To link to a document - Browse your computer or the network for a document you want to link. The **Look in:** dropdown **C** displays the folder you are currently viewing. Double-click the document you want to link to. The **Insert Hyperlink** box closes and Word creates the link.

To link to a Web page - Click the **Browse the Web** icon in the upper-right corner **D** to open your default web browser. Go to the web page you want to link to and then go back to the **Insert Hyperlink** dialog box. Word adds the address in your web browser to the **Address** text box **E**. To see links to Web pages you have recently visited, click the **Browsed Pages** button **F**. Click any of these URLs to add it to the **Address** text box.

- **Place in This Document G**: Select this option if you are creating a link to help readers jump around in a long document. Within a document, Word can create links to either headings or bookmarks

- **Create New Document H**: Select this option to create a hyperlink to a document you have not created yet. When you click **Create New Document**, the **Insert Hyperlink** box changes. Type the name of the new document you want to create in the **Name of new document** text box. Click **OK** to save your new document.

CONTINUE

- **E-mail Address** I : Select this option to create a mail to hyperlink in your document. The **Edit Hyperlink** box changes and you can now type the e-mail address that you want hyperlinked .

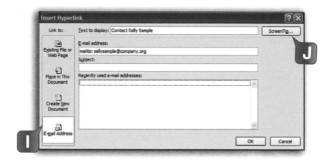

4. Click the **ScreenTip** button J to add a screen tip to the hyperlink. This is text that appears in a box when the user hovers over the hyperlink within a web browser. This is optional.

5. The **Text to Display** text box  is where you edit the text that is hyperlinked. By default, the text or object you selected in Step 1 will appear in this box.

6. When edits are complete, click **OK**  to apply.

7. The text you highlighted is now blue and underlined, indicating that it is an active hyperlink.

Click Here to Visit Vendor Website
Ctrl+Click to follow link

Kansas City Web Developer

8. Users can **CTRL+click** on the hyperlink to follow the link.

 Quickest Click: Select the text to be linked, then right-click and select **Hyperlink**  from the menu.

 Caution: If you edit the text in the **Text to Display** box, make sure that the text you've entered fits within the context of document. You may have to go back into your document and review/edit to verify.

35 | Mark a Point in a Document for Future Access

Difficulty: ●○○○

PROBLEM You have created a detailed reference guide. You want to create a way for certain items within the document to be easily and quickly referenced—from a Table of Contents or from other parts of the document.

SOLUTION Use a **Bookmark** or a **Cross Reference** to mark text so that you and your reader can quickly get to it. You can create a named bookmark to indicate a certain place in the document and then reference that bookmark's name in a variety of ways, including cross-referencing or linking. Bookmarks can be created in any section of a document and can reference a specific location, paragraphs of text, or objects.

Bookmarks are most typically used for navigation and cross-references. But you may also want to use them as a Hypertext anchor. When you create a hyperlink to a specific point within your document, Word needs something to anchor the link to. This can be a heading or a bookmark that you have already created.

 What Microsoft Calls It: Bookmarks

 Step-by-Step

Create a Bookmark

1. Position the cursor in the place that the bookmark will be inserted **A**.

    *   To bookmark a paragraph, position the cursor at the beginning of that paragraph.

    *   To bookmark an image or other object, select the image or object.

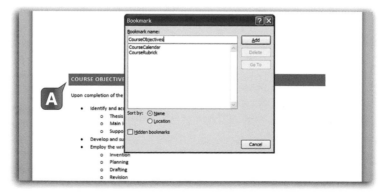

2. On the **Insert** tab, in the **Links** group, select **Bookmark** **B** to launch the Bookmark dialog box.

3. In the **Bookmark name** text box **C**, type a name for the bookmark.

   • Bookmark names can be up to 40 characters and *can* include letters and/or numbers.

   • Spaces and symbols *cannot* be used.

4. Click **Add** **D** to create the bookmark.

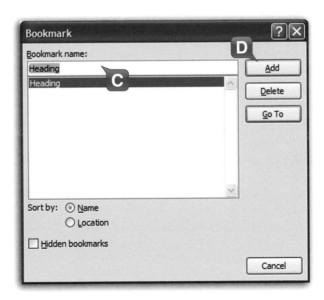

Step-by-Step

Go to your Bookmarks

1. On the **Home** tab, in the **Editing** group, click **Find**  E to open the **Find and Replace** dialog box.

2. Click on the **Go To** tab **F**.

3. In the **Go to what:** box **G**, click on **Bookmark** to bring up a dropdown list **H** of all the bookmarks you have created in the document. Select the one you want, then click **Go To** **I**. ✵

Step-by-Step

Create a Cross-Reference

Cross-references direct the reader to related information (photos, charts, tables, or other parts of the document) located elsewhere in the document.

1. Select the text that starts the cross-reference in the document.

2. On the **References** tab, in the **Captions** group, click the **Cross-Reference** button **J**.

3. Click the **References type** dropdown arrow 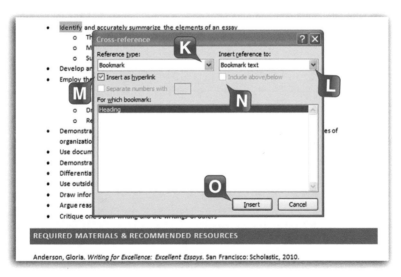 and select the type of reference you're linking to (bookmark, footnote, heading, etc.).

4. Click the **Insert reference to** dropdown arrow and select the type of data (page, paragraph number, etc.) that you want to reference.

5. Click the specific item that you want referenced.

6. To let users click to this item, select the **Insert as hyperlink** check box.

7. To include data regarding the relative position of the referenced item, select the Include above/below check box.

8. Click **Insert**.

9. Repeat steps for additional cross-references.

10. Click **Close** to finish.

Quickest Click: Use **CTRL+G** to open the **Find and Replace** dialog box.

36 Create a Table of Contents

Difficulty: ●●○○

PROBLEM You have created a detailed proposal for a client. Since the document is split into separate sections, you want the client to easily find the information he needs without having to scroll through the document page by page.

SOLUTION A **Table of Contents** allows you to quickly find a section and page number, then go immediately to it without having to scroll or page through the document. You can easily create a **Table of Contents** by applying preset Heading Styles to your text. Microsoft Word 2010 searches for headings that match the style that you have applied, and inserts the heading text into the **Table of Contents**.

See Also: Apply Styles to Text

Step-by-Step

Word 2010, by default, uses Heading 1 as the first-level entry in the Table of Contents. Subheadings, using Heading 2 and so forth, would appear in subsequent order.

1. Select the text (formatted as a heading or title/subtitle) that you want to appear in the Table of Contents **A**.

2. On the **Home** tab, in the **Styles** group, select a style for the heading **B**.

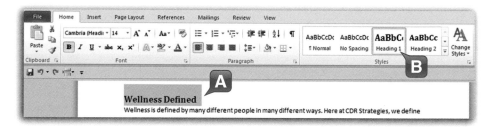

3. Repeat these steps (select heading and a heading style) for all the titles/subtitles you want to appear in the **Table of Contents**.

4. Place the cursor in the area you want the **Table of Contents** to appear. This is typically the beginning of the document or in between a cover page and the start of the text.

5. On the **References** tab, in the **Table of Contents** group, click **Table of Contents** **C**.

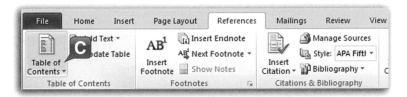

6. Click on an **Automatic Table** style to select it **D** or click the **Insert Table of Contents...** menu option **E** to open the **Table of Contents** dialog box **F**. Set your preferences in the dialog box, then click **OK** to insert the **Table of Contents** into your document.

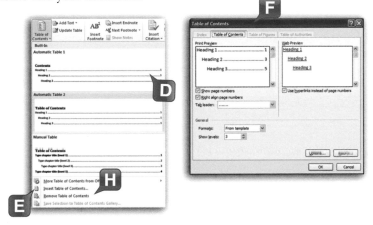

7. As you edit your document and add or delete text and headings, the page numbers and items for the Table of Contents may change. To update the Table of Contents, select the **Table of Contents** object in your document and click the **Update Table** button **G** located at the top of the object.

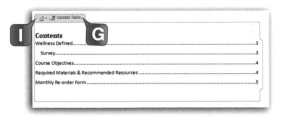

CONTINUE

8. Click the radio button beside the option to update the entire table or just the page numbers. If heading text has been added or deleted, choose to update the entire table so those edits will be accounted for in the Table of Contents.

9. To remove a Table of Contents from your document, click the **Table of Contents** button **C** on the **References** tab in the **Table of Contents** group and click **Remove Table of Contents** **H** from the dropdown menu.

   You can also remove a Table of Contents by clicking on the **Table of Contents** menu tab at the top of an active Table of Contents object **I** and then clicking **Remove Table of Contents**.

Hot Tip: Hyperlink your Table of Contents headings to the sections they reference. This allows you to easily and quickly access those sections of your document. See the **Insert a Hyperlink** tip for more details.

Quickest Click: To change the style of the Table of Contents in your document, click the **Table of Contents** button on the **References** tab in the **Table of Contents** group and select a different style option. This will simply replace the current Table of Contents style with the new style.

Bright Idea: If you want to include text in the Table of Contents that is not formatted as a heading, select the text and click **Add Text** button **J** in the **Table of Contents** group on the **References** tab.

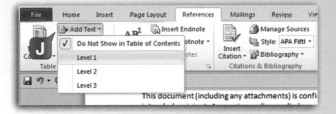

37 | Create an Index

Difficulty: ●●○○

PROBLEM You have been asked to create a technical user guide for customers. The customers have indicated that they will not read the user guide from front to back, but instead will look for the items they need and go directly to the pages they are interested in.

SOLUTION An index lists words and topics that appear in a document, as well as their page numbers. An index can be created for individual words, for topics that span multiple pages, or for items that refer to other terms in the document. An index is useful when publishing a large document, such as a detailed report, a technical user guide, or a book manuscript. The index helps readers find a specific topic or term easily and quickly. Creating an index is a three-part process: first, items for entry are marked; second, a design for your index is selected; and last, the index is built.

See Also: Mark a Point in a Document for Future Access

Step-by-Step

Mark and Format Entries for Index

1. In the document, highlight a word or phrase to be indexed.

2. On the **References** tab, in the **Index** group, click **Mark Entry** Ⓐ to launch the **Mark Index Entry** dialog box. ⚡

3. In the **Mark Entry** dialog box, verify the content in the **Main Entry:** text box Ⓑ. *Note: The text does not have to appear exactly the same way it appears in the document. You can highlight an abbreviation, for example, but display the full term in the index.*

4. Create a **Subentry** 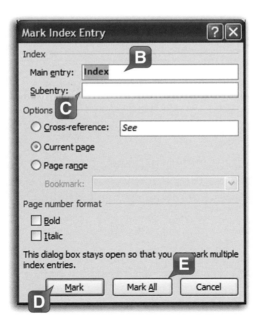, or **Cross-reference,** to another entry. These are optional fields.

   - **Cross-reference**: Refers to another index entry. For example, select the word "house" and then type "home" in the cross-reference box. The index entry looks like this: "house, See home."

   - **Current page**: Use to index individual words, phrases, or symbols.

   - **Page range**: Use for entries that span more than one page. Select **Page range**, and then select a bookmark from the **Bookmark** dropdown menu.

   *Note: Before you can mark a **Page range** index, you must create a bookmark. Select the text and click **ALT+N+K**.*

5. Format the page numbers that will appear in the index by clicking the **Bold** or **Italic** check box under **Page number format.**

6. Mark the index entry by clicking the **Mark** button D. To mark all appearances of the text in the entire document, click the **Mark All** button E.

7. To mark additional index entries, follow steps 1-6 until complete.

Step-by-Step

Build the Index

1. Place cursor where the index will appear. Typically, this is on a new page at the end of a document.

2. On the **References** tab, in the **Index** group, click **Insert Index** **F** to launch the Index dialog box.

3. Select a design in the **Formats** dropdown **G**. A preview will appear in the preview pane above **H**.

4. Click **OK** **I**.

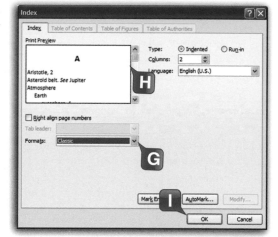

Step-by-Step

Update the Index

If you marked additional text and made changes to your document after your index was created, follow these steps to update the index:

1. Place your cursor anywhere within the index.

2. Click **Update Index** in the **Index** group on the **References** tab **J**.

3. Microsoft Word will re-read all the index entries to include any changes. ⚡

Quickest Click: To open the **Mark Index Entry** dialog box, press **Alt+Shift+X**.

 Quickest Click: To update the index, press the **F9** Key or **ALT+S+D**.

 Hot Tip: To format the index text, select the text in the **Main entry** or **Subentry** box. Right-click and select **Font**. Select the formatting.

 Caution: Look out for words that appear often but lack relevance.

 Bright Idea: To select a range of text that spans for several pages, click **Bookmark** on the **Insert** tab in the **Links** group. In the **Bookmark name** box **K**, type a name. Click **Add** **L**. Mark the entry using steps above.

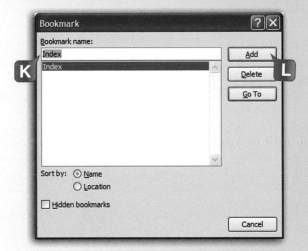

38 Insert a Footnote or Endnote

Difficulty: ●○○○

PROBLEM You have created a long document that references several sources of information. You want to reference these sources but do not want to create a long, formal bibliography at the end of your document. Instead, you want to display these less rigorous references at the bottom of each page or at the end of the document.

SOLUTION Footnotes and endnotes are ways to cite sources in a document. The difference between a footnote and an endnote is location. Footnotes are displayed at the bottom of the page that the reference appears. Endnotes are displayed at the end of the document or section.

Step-by-Step

Insert a Footnote

1. Place your cursor after the text you want your footnote to reference.

2. On the **References** tab, in the **Footnotes** group, click the **Insert Footnote**  button. Word inserts a reference mark at the insertion point and then jumps to the bottom of the page and places a footnote reference.

3. Type the footnote text.

Step-by-Step

Insert an Endnote

1. Place your cursor after the text you want your endnote to reference.

2. On the **References** tab, in the **Footnotes** group, select **Insert Endnote** **B**.

3. Word inserts a reference mark at the insertion point and then jumps to the end of the document and places a new endnote reference.

4. Type the endnote text.

Step-by-Step

Format a Footnote or Endnote

1. Place your cursor in the section where you want to change the footnote or endnote format.

2. On the **References** tab, in the **Footnotes** group, click the **Footnote & Endnote** dialog box launcher **C**.

3. Make your adjustments in the **Footnote** and **Endnote** dialog box:

   To select the way footnotes and endnotes are numbered, choose a style from the **Number format** menu **D**.

   To change the starting point, click the **Start at** up or down arrows **E**.

4. Click **Apply change to** and select **Whole document** **F**.

5. Click **Apply** **G** and then click **Cancel** **H** to close.

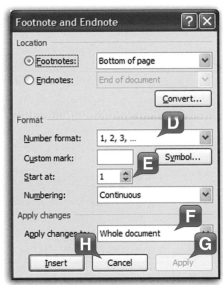

39 | Correctly Cite Sources in a Document

Difficulty: ●○○○

PROBLEM You are writing a long paper or report that references a variety of books, articles, and other resources. You need to create a works cited page to correctly cite the sources used in your document.

SOLUTION Create a bibliography. A bibliography typically appears at the end of a document and provides information about the sources of your cited references. When you create a bibliography, you can choose a standard style, (such as APA or MLA), which is widely used in organizations and universities. To create a bibliography, you will first enter the source data (such as the title, author, and date of publication) and then cite them in the document with just a few clicks.

>  **What Microsoft Calls It:** Insert Citation; Manage Sources

 Step-by-Step

Entering Sources

1. Select a citation style from the **Style** dropdown list in the **Citations & Bibliography** group **A** on the **References** tab.

2. Click the **Manage Sources** button **B** to open the **Source Manager** dialog box.

3. Click **New C**.

4. In the **Create Source** dialog box, open the **Type of Source** dropdown list **D** and select type (i.e. Book, Journal Article, etc.).

5. Enter the Author's name into the **Author** text box **E** in one of two formats:
   - First Middle Last
   - Last, First Middle
   - If there is more than one author, separate names with semicolons.

   OR-

   You can click the **Edit** button **F** to enter each part of the name as prompted in the **Edit Name** dialog box.
   - If there is only one author, click **OK**.
   - If there are multiple authors, click **Add** **G** after entering each name and click **OK** **H** when complete.

   If the author is an organization, click the **Corporate Author** **I** check box and enter the organization's name.

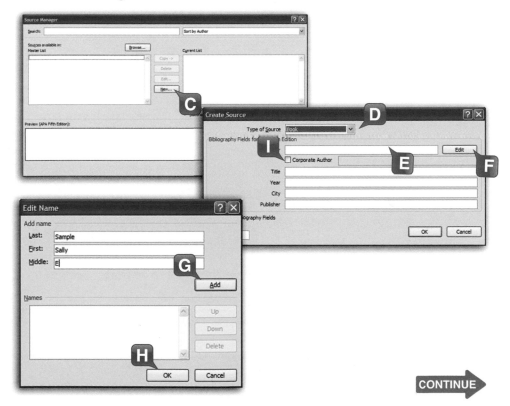

6. Complete any additional fields required for the selected source type.

7. Click **OK** to return to the **Source Manager** dialog box.

8. Create another new source by clicking **New** or click **Close** to finish.

Step-by-Step

Insert In-Line References

An in-line reference to a source is inserted using parentheses. The style of these references differs based upon the citation style you are using as well as the source type. These generally include at least the name of the Author, and often the Year, Title, or Page Number.

1. Place cursor in the position where your citation should appear.

2. On the **References** tab, in the **Citations & Bibliography** group, click **Insert Citation** J.

3. A menu lists all the sources in the current document.

4. Click the source being cited.

5. A reference to the source will be added as a field K.

> to the Lab for Popular Studies at the University of Lorenzia, there is a
> thing A and thing B. (Simple, 1999) When you look closely at the resear
> needs to be done to address this phenomenon. According to the Lab
> sity of

Step-by-Step

Generate Bibliography

1. Place the cursor where the bibliography should appear (typically on a new page at the end of your document).

2. On the **References** tab, in the **Citations & Bibliography** group, click **Bibliography** .

3. Click the gallery entry that best represents the bibliography you want to create.

4. Click **Insert Bibliography.**

Bright Idea: If you're writing a document and need to cite a source, but don't have the details at hand, you can create a temporary placeholder for the source and then complete the details later in the Source Manager. This allows for maximum productivity. Just remember to name your placeholder something that you can easily identify later.

40 | Create a Table of Authorities

Difficulty: ●●○○

PROBLEM You have created a lengthy legal document for a partnering law firm to review prior to an upcoming case. You need to create a table of authorities to reference past cases and rulings in the document for faster and more efficient review.

SOLUTION A Table of Authorities is a list of references (such as cases, statutes, and rulings) in a legal document and the page numbers where the references appear. Start by marking the citations. Citations are different from footnotes and bibliography entries because they are almost exclusively used by the legal industry. Word simplifies the process of adding citations in-line with the text and then bundles them into a master reference called the Table of Authorities.

Step-by-Step

Mark Citations

1. Select the first relevant citation in the document .

   - For example, select "Smith v. Jones, 257 U.S 198 (1972)"

2. On the **References** tab, in the **Table of Authorities** group, click **Mark Citation B** to open the **Mark Citation** dialog box.

3. In the **Mark Citation** dialog box, edit the text if necessary **C**.

4. Open the **Category** dropdown menu **D** and select the type of citation (cases, statutes, etc.)

5. In the **Short Citation** box, enter a short version of the citation. The default is a copy of the selected text **E**.

6. Click **Mark** **F**.

7. The selected text now appears in the **Long Citation** box **G**. 💧

8. To mark another citation, click **Next Citation**.

9. Repeat steps until all citations have been marked.

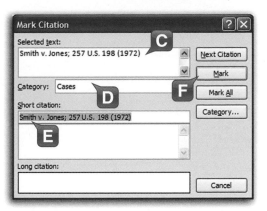

CONTINUE

Step-by-Step

Create Table of Authorities

1. Position the cursor where the table should appear.

2. On the **References** tab, in the **Table of Authorities** group, click **Insert Table of Authorities**  to open the Table of Authorities dialog box.

3. In the **Table of Authorities** dialog box, setting options are as follows:

   - **Use Passim**: When listing citations that appear frequently in the same document, it is standard to substitute the word *passim* for the multiple references. Word, by default, uses *passim* after at least five references to the same citation appear. Uncheck the checkbox if you want to display the actual page numbers in each instance instead.

   - **Keep Original Formatting**: Some citations contain character formatting that carries, by default, into the Table of Authorities. If you do not want the formatting to carry over, uncheck the checkbox.

   - **Tab leader**: Select the leader type or "none."

   - **Formats**: Select one of the style sets or use **From Template** to match the style set that the document uses.

   - **Category**: This defaults to **ALL** 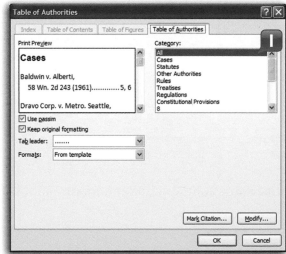. Narrow this down by selecting.

   - Click **Modify** to modify the styles used for the **Table of Authorities**. This is optional.

4. Click **OK** to apply modifications and create the table of authorities.

Cases

Smith v Jones, 257 U.S. 198 (1972)..1

Hot Tip: If you want Word to scan the entire document and mark all references to the same citation, short and long, click **Mark All**.

Caution: If you add, delete, move, or edit a citation or other text in a document, remember to update the table of authorities. For example, move a citation to a different page, you need to make sure that the table of authorities reflects the new page number.

To update the table of authorities, click to the left of it and click the **Update Table** button in the **Table of Authorities** group on the **References** tab. Don't modify entries directly in the finished table of authorities; if you do, your changes will be lost when you update the table of authorities.

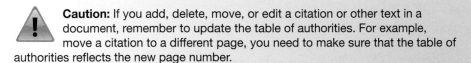

41 Customize the Quick Access Toolbar and Status Bar

Difficulty: ●●○○

PROBLEM There are several actions and commands you use frequently, but they are spread across multiple tabs and often several clicks deep. It would be helpful if they were available in one convenient menu.

SOLUTION The **Quick Access Toolbar** is a row of buttons in the top-left corner of the Word window. This toolbar can be repositioned either above or below the Ribbon and can be customized. Buttons can be added, removed, or rearranged. The **Status Bar** is the bar at the bottom of the Word window. The status bar contains items such as page status, word count, page view buttons, and a zoom slide button.

Customizing the Quick Access Toolbar or the Status Bar allows you to quickly perform tasks that are not necessarily available through a shortcut key or available by clicking the Ribbon. Since utilizing this customization option is a highly individualized task, the variations are limitless.

See Also: Record and Play Back a Series of Actions

 Step-by-Step

Customize the Quick Access Toolbar

1. Click the **Customize Quick Access Toolbar button** Ⓐ to the right of the **Quick Access Toolbar**, at the top left corner of your window to open the dropdown menu Ⓑ.

2. If the command you want to add to the **Quick Access Toolbar** is on the default list of common commands, then click it. A checkmark will appear by the command in the menu and the command's icon will appear in the toolbar at the top of your window.

3. To add any command to the toolbar, click the **More Commands** menu option Ⓒ to open the **Word Options** dialog box.

4. Open the **Choose commands from:** dropdown menu 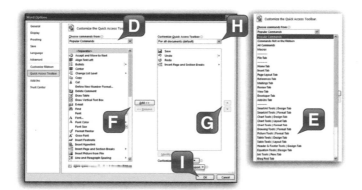 and make a selection:

- Popular commands: This includes commands that Word users most frequently use in the **Quick Access Toolbar**, such as **Save**, **Open**, **New, and Print Preview**.

- Commands not in the ribbon: This includes features that were either available in a previous version of Word or only pertain to specific types of projects and are less frequently used. Microsoft did not put these commands on the 2010 ribbon.

- All commands: This includes a list of all available commands.

- Macros: This includes a list of all available macros.

- You can also choose from commands as they are organized on the ribbon. Click the **Drawing Tools | Format Tab** option to see all the commands that are visible only when an image or photograph is selected.

5. Select a command from the left pane, then click **Add F**. The command will be added to the **Quick Access Toolbar** pane with your existing choices. Add more commands as desired.

6. To arrange the order you would like the commands to appear, click on the **Up/ Down** arrows **G** to the right of the toolbar pane to move the commands up and down (right or left in your toolbar).

7. Click on the **Customize Quick Access Toolbar** dropdown **H** to choose whether you wish these settings to apply to all windows you open in Word, or only for the document you are currently working on.

8. Click **OK I**. Your new commands will appear in your **Quick Access Toolbar**.

Step-by-Step

Customize the Status Bar

1. Right-click the Status Bar **J**.

2. A menu opens with check marks next to the displayed items **K**. Click an item to toggle it on or off.

3. Checked items will be active and visible on the **Status Bar**.

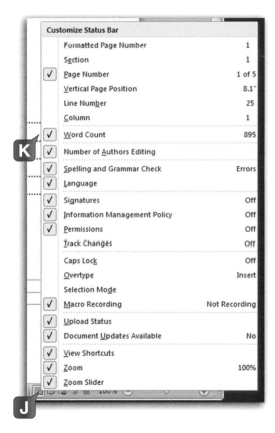

42 Create Templates

Difficulty: ●●●○

PROBLEM You send daily updates that need to include your organization's branding, colors, fonts, logo, and corporate tagline. Currently, you save an old formatted document and do a "Save As" to edit all the text within the document. This is proving to be ineffective, as you have made mistakes by not deleting all the old text appropriately. You want a way to make the creation of these documents simple and clean.

SOLUTION Templates are documents that are predesigned and preformatted to serve as the foundations for other documents. Each template is made up of styles that have common design elements, such as fonts, sizes, colors, and layout. Templates can also contain styles and even preset text, if desired.

See Also: Save a Document to the Appropriate File Format, Insert and Manage Stored Document Components

Step-by-Step

Create a Template

Enter all your necessary information into a new document, such as formatting and graphics. You can enter generic text as a placeholder. However, this is a matter of preference. Some people prefer to work with a clean slate to prevent errors. This decision should be driven by the content you are working with and your preferences.

1. Click the **File** tab.

2. Click the **Save As** button **A** on the **File** tab to launch the **Save As** dialog box.

3. In the **Save As** dialog box, browse to the folder(s) where templates are saved:
   - On a computer running Windows 7, click the **Templates** folder at the top of the folder list under **Microsoft Word**.
   - On a computer running Windows Visa, click **Templates** folder under **Favorite Links.**
   - On a computer running Windows XP (shown in examples), click **Trusted Templates** B under **Save in**.

   Note: You can save your template to any location on your computer, or on your network if the template will be used by others in your organization.

4. In the **Save As Type** dropdown menu C, select from the following template types:
   - Word Template: Select this to create a template for Word 2010.
   - Word Macro-Enabled Template: Select this to create a template for Word 2010 with macros.
   - Word 97-2003 Template: Select this to create a template for Word versions 97 through 2003.

5. Click **Save** D.

CONTINUE

Step-by-Step

Use a Template to Create New Document

1. Click the **New** tab **E** on the **File** tab.

2. Click **My Templates** **F** to open the **New** dialog box **G**. ⚠

3. Click on your saved custom template, then click **OK** to open a new document.

Caution: If you saved your template in a folder other than the default Word **Templates** folder, you will not see your template under the **My templates** button on the **New** tab. To open a template from another folder, click **Open H** in Step 1, then select your template format from the **Files of type** dropdown in the **Open** dialog box. Browse to the folder where your template is saved.

Hot Tip: When you open a template, the template itself does not change as you enter content. Word starts a new document that contains the formatting, graphics, and text settings contained in the template. To save your new document, choose **Save As**.

43 Locate and Substitute Words, Formatting, Terms, and Objects in a Document

Difficulty: ●●○○

PROBLEM You realize that you have text in your document that you need to change. You have spelled the name "Ann" (one of your customers) incorrectly throughout your 50 page document. You need to replace her name with the correct spelling, "Anne." You do not want to do it manually, because you might miss an occurrence within the document.

SOLUTION There are a variety of ways to locate content in a document. The Find feature helps locate instances of a specified string of text. It can also locate specific formatting, or a non-printing symbol or code. You can search for tabs or paragraph breaks as well as phone numbers or names beginning with certain letters. The Replace feature then takes the next step of replacing the found item with a different text string. There are a variety of useful functions in the Editing tool.

In Word 2010, the Find feature has been integrated with the new Navigation pane that offers you a variety of ways to browse and move through your document.

 What Microsoft Calls It: Find and Replace

Step-by-Step

Basic Find and Replace

1. On the **Home** tab in the **Editing** group, click **Find**. The **Navigation** pane  **A** will open to the left of your document pane.

2. Type the text string you are looking for into the **Search Document** box **B** and press the **ENTER** key on your keyboard.

3. Word will highlight matches for your search in the current page on the document pane **C** and generate a list of matches in the **Navigation** pane **D**. Click on any of the results to jump to that page.

4. To replace your search phrase with new text, click the dropdown arrow **E** to the right of the **Search** box and select **Advanced Find** **F** from the menu to open the **Find and Replace** dialog box.

5. Click on the **Replace** tab **G**. Your search text will be pre-filled into the **Find what** text box **H**.

6. Enter the text you want to replace original in the **Replace with** box **I**.

7. Click **Replace** **J**. Word will highlight the next match it finds. Click **Replace** again to make the change or **Find Next** **K** to skip that match. Click **Replace All** to allow Word to replace all matches without reviewing each change.

8. Repeat until Word has finished searching the document. 🔥

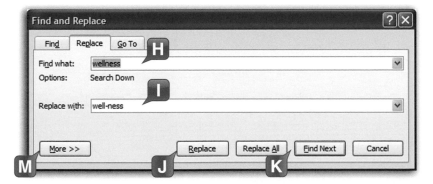

Step-by-Step

Find and Replace Formatting in the Document

The **Find and Replace Formatting in the Document** feature allows you find text or other elements with a specific font, paragraph, tab, language, frame, style, or highlight attributes or to add that feature to text and objects. The **Reading Highlight** button highlights items found to make them easier to read. 🔥

1. Open the **Find and Replace** dialog box as described above, or click the dropdown arrow on the **Find** combo button in the **Editing** group on the **Home** tab and select **Advanced Find** **L**.

2. On the **Replace** tab, type the text you want to find.

3. Place your cursor.

    • Putting it in the **Find What** text box allows you to search for text formatted in the way you specify.

    • Putting it in the **Replace With** text box allows you to replace the searched-for text with the formatting you specify.

4. In the **Find and Replace** dialog box, click the **More** button **M** to display additional **Find** options **N**.

5. Click the **Format** button **O** to open the formatting menu.

6. Select the type of formatting to specify. For example, to specify character formatting such as a font, click **Font**. A corresponding dialog box will open.

7. Specify the type of formatting you want to find.

8. Click **OK**. *(Note: The dialog box and options will differ based on the formatting menu item you choose.)*

9. In the **Find and Replace** dialog box, descriptive text appears under the **Find what** box identifying the formatting chosen for the **Find** action **P**.

10. Continue the find and/or replace options as normal.

Step-by-Step

Find and Replace Special Characters

The **Find and Replace Special Characters** feature is useful if you want to replace all single paragraph breaks in a document with double paragraph breaks.

1. In the **Find and Replace** dialog box, click the **More** button to display additional **Find** options.

2. Click the **Special** button to open a menu of special characters to choose from.

3. Select the special character you want to find. Word will put the text code for the character in the **Find what** text box **Q**.

4. Continue the **Find** and/or **Replace** operations as normal.

 Caution: Replace All is a quick way to substitute text throughout the entire document. However, you must be careful that the string of text does not exist as a part of any other words in the document. For example, you are using the **Find and Replace** function to replace the misspelled name Ann with Anne. If you have the word Annully in your document, the Replace All function will change your word to Anneuity. To correct for this, make sure you choose to replace "Ann " (with a space after the second "n") with "Anne " (with a space after the "e"). This will allow you to make the replacement without introducing additional errors.

Hot Tip: If you think you have overused a word, and you want to quickly search the document to find all instances of the word, select the word in the document. Click the **Find** button in the **Editing** group on the **Home** tab. Word will highlight all instances of the word and pre-fill it into the **Search Document** box. To cancel highlighting, click the **Close** button to the right of the search box **R**.

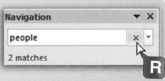

44 | Use AutoCorrect to Save Time and Prevent Errors

Difficulty: ●●○○

PROBLEM You often mistype the name of your organization's research facility, Joulette Thomatican Laboratory.

SOLUTION AutoCorrect is a function that automatically replaces all instances of a certain text string with another. By setting **AutoCorrect** options, you can save time by automatically correcting typos within a document. In this example, set the AutoCorrect option so you can type *JT Lab* and Word will autocorrect it to display *Joulette Thomatican Laboratory*. Because the corrections are made automatically, you will not need to edit these later.

Step-by-Step

Setting AutoCorrect Options

1. On the **File** tab, click the **Options** button  to launch the **Word Options** dialog box.

2. Click the **Proofing** tab **B**, then click the **AutoCorrect Options** button **C** to launch the **AutoCorrect** dialog box.

3. The top portion of the AutoCorrect tab contains check boxes for enabling/disabling certain features.

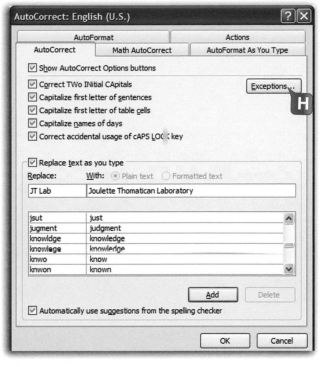

- **Show AutoCorrect Options Buttons:** Clear this to prevent the AutoCorrect Options button from appearing after an AutoCorrect action.

- **Correct TWo INitial CApitals:** If a word starts out with two capital letters and then switches to lowercase, AutoCorrect will lowercase the second letter.

- **Capitalize First Letter of Sentences:** AutoCorrect will capitalize the first letter of the first word that comes at the beginning of a paragraph or after a sentence-ending punctuation mark.

- **Capitalize First Letter of Table Cells:** AutoCorrect will capitalize the first letter of the first word in each table cell.

- **Capitalize Names of Days:** AutoCorrect will capitalize days of the week, such as Monday, Tuesday, etc.

- **Correct Accidental Usage of CAPS LOCK Key:** When this feature is enabled, AutoCorrect notices when you have left the Caps Lock on and will turn it off and correct the text that was accidentally capitalized.

Step-by-Step

Change, Remove, or Add an AutoCorrect Entry

While AutoCorrect entries, in general, are useful and save you time, there are some settings that might actually work against you. For example, a frequent troublemaker is the AutoCorrect entry for the copyright symbol. Those who use (c) to represent anything other than the Copyright symbol are often frustrated by this auto-correction.

To edit an entry:

1. Click the **File** tab.

2. Click the **Options** button **A** to launch the **Word Options** dialog box.

3. Click the **Proofing** tab **B**, then click the **AutoCorrect Options** button **C** to launch the **AutoCorrect** dialog box.

4. Scroll through the **Replace Text as You Type** list **D** to locate entries that you want to edit or delete.

5. Click on the entry and it will appear in the **Replace** and **With** boxes **E**. Edit the text in either box to change the entry or click the **Delete** button to remove it completely.

6. To add a new entry, fill in the text you want to type and the text that should replace it in the **Replace** and **With** boxes, then click **Add** **F**.

7. Click **OK** **G**.

Hot Tip: To create exceptions for some of the features, click the **Exceptions** button . The **AutoCorrect Exceptions** dialog box opens. For each tab, **Add** and **Delete** to manage the list of exceptions.

Bright Idea: You can insert blocks of text that you type frequently by adding text to the **Replace text as you type** list. For example, if you frequently type "Equal Employment Opportunity Commission," you might consider adding "EOCC" to the **Replace** list and "Equal Employment Opportunity Commission" to the **With** list. Each time you type EOCC, it will be AutoCorrected to display the full text, saving time and opportunity for errors.

45 Customize Spellcheck and Grammar Check Options

Difficulty: ●●○○

PROBLEM While working on Word projects, you are distracted by notations alerting you to spelling and grammar errors as you type. You want to monitor spelling and grammar in the document creation process.

SOLUTION Customize the spelling and grammar checker by selecting specific options to employ (or not) as Word checks document's spelling and grammar.

See Also: Create Custom Spellcheck Lists for Documents and Projects

 Step-by-Step

Customize Spellcheck Settings

1. On the **File** tab, click the **Options** button **A** to launch the **Word Options** dialog box.

2. Click the **Proofing** tab **B**.

3. Basic spelling options are found in the **When correcting spelling in Microsoft Office Programs** section **C**. These apply to all Office applications, such as Word, Excel, and PowerPoint.

4. To set options for Word only, review options in the **When correcting spelling and grammar in Word** section **D**:

   - **Check spelling as you type**: Turn this off to stop Word from checking spelling (and red-underlining words).

   - **Use contextual spelling:** Turn this off to stop Word from blue-underlining words that might be used improperly in the current context.

   - **Mark grammar errors as you type:** Turn this off to stop Word from checking grammar (green underlining words and phrases).

   - **Recheck Document:** Click this button to run the spelling and grammar check again after changing the grammar settings to see if any additional errors or concerns are identified.

- **Show readability statistics:**
Turn this on to display a box
with readability information
at the end of a spelling and
grammar check with the
Spelling and Grammar
dialog box.

- **Writing Style:** Set the
level of grammar check
you require. Elect to check
grammar only or to include
other style issues such as
contractions, commonly
misspelled words, fragments,
etc.

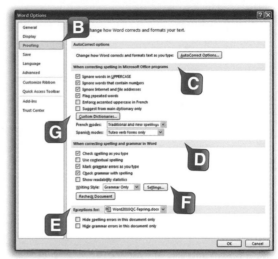

5. The **Exceptions** for section **E** allows you to select exceptions for any active
    document including the following:

6. **Hide spelling errors in this document only:** This does not turn off the
    spellchecking as you type. However, it prevents the red underlines from appearing
    on the screen.

7. **Hide grammar errors in this document only:** This does not turn off the
    grammar checking as you type. However, it prevents the green underlines from
    appearing on the screen.

Step-by-Step

Customize Grammar Settings

1. Click the **File** tab.

2. Click the **Options** button  to launch the **Word Options** dialog box.

3. Click the **Proofing** tab **B**.

4. In the **When Correcting Spelling and Grammar in Word** section **C**, click the **Settings** button **F** to open the **Grammar Settings** dialog box.

5. In the **Writing style** dropdown menu, select the writing style you want to customize (Grammar only or Grammar & Style).

   - **Comma required before last list item:** When you have three or more items in a list, some writing styles prescribe a comma between the last two. However, in other writing styles, the comma is omitted. Choices are either *Always* or *Never.*

   - **Punctuation required with quotes:** Some writing styles prescribe that punctuation should fall within the quotation mark when both occur at the end of a sentence. In other writing styles, the punctuation falls outside of the quotes. Choices are *Don't Check, Inside,* or *Outside. Inside* is most commonly used.

   - **Spaces required between sentences:** Some writing styles prescribe one blank space between sentences while others prescribe two. Options are one or two.

Step-by-Step

Manage Custom Spelling Dictionaries

1. Click the **File** tab.

2. Click the **Options** button  to launch the **Word Options** dialog box.

3. Click the **Proofing** tab **B** .

4. Click the **Custom Dictionaries** button **G**.

5. Select a custom dictionary from the list or add a new one.

6. In the **Custom Dictionaries** dialog box **H**, you can edit word lists, adding to and/or deleting words from a custom dictionary.

7. Click **OK** when finished.

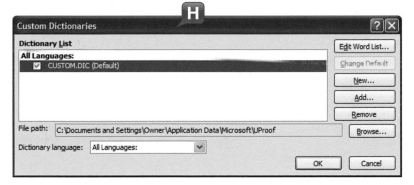

46 | Create Custom Spellcheck Lists for Documents and Projects

Difficulty: ●●●○

PROBLEM When creating Word documents, your name is flagged as a misspelled word.

SOLUTION Add your name to a custom dictionary so it is no longer marked as a misspelling. Creating a custom dictionary permits you to edit the word list and add specific words. Terms added to the custom dictionary will not be flagged by the spellchecker in your Word 2010 projects.

What Microsoft Calls It: Custom Dictionaries

Step-by-Step

Edit Custom Dictionaries

1. Click the **File** tab.

2. Click the **Options** button  to launch the **Word Options** dialog box.

3. Click the **Proofing** tab **B**.

4. Click the **Custom Dictionaries** button **C** to launch the **Custom Dictionaries** dialog box.

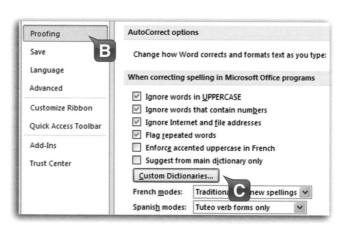

5. Select a custom dictionary from the **Dictionary List** D or add a new one.

6. Click the **Edit Word List** button E. A dialog box appears listing all the words currently in that dictionary.

7. To add a new word, type it in the **Word(s)** box F and click **Add** G. ⚠

8. To delete a word, select it and click **Delete** H.

9. To clear the entire dictionary, click **Delete All** I.

10. Click **OK** on all open dialog boxes when finished editing the custom dictionary.
    ⚡ 💧

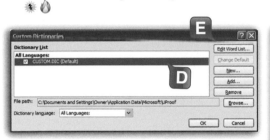
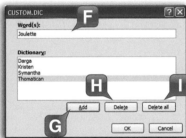

 Caution: Words can be no longer than 64 characters.

Hot Tip: You can create project-specific custom dictionaries. The more words you add to a dictionary, especially foreign words, names and acronyms, the more likely it is that a true typographical error will slip through the cracks. Creating custom dictionaries for each project can minimize the number of words added to any given list. This is especially useful for authors and those in legal professions.

 Quickest Click: You can add an entire list of words at one time to a custom dictionary. This is useful when you have a list of frequently used terms, not included in the main dictionary—such as employee names, product names, or internal acronyms.

47 | Record and Play Back a Series of Actions

Difficulty: ●●○○

PROBLEM Every week a report is pulled from the tracking system and the information from the report needs to be translated into a summary document. The report, by default, displays the dollar currency symbol as the letter C. So, each week, you have to do a search and replace on hundreds of pages to edit this information.

SOLUTION Since you perform this manual action frequently, creating a macro would save time and money. A macro is a sequence of actions that Word will execute when you run it. Macros enable you to automate a variety of operations that typically would be completed manually.

> **What Microsoft Calls It:** Macros

Step-by-Step

Create a Macro

1. On the **View** tab **A**, in the **Macros** group, click the lower half of the **Macros** button **B**.

2. Select **Record Macro.** ✷

3. In the **Record Macro** dialog box, type a name for the macro **C**. The macro name must start with a letter and contain no spaces.

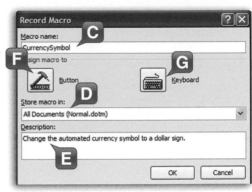

4. From the **Store macro in** dropdown menu **D**, select the template or document where you want to store the macro.

   - **All Documents**: Select this to have the macro available anytime you use Word.

   - **Documents Based On**: Select this to have the macro available any time you use a document that is based on the current document.

   - **document-name.docx (document):** Select this to have the macro available in the current document only.

5. In the **Description** box **E**, enter a description of the macro that will help you and others easily identify which actions the macro completes (optional).

6. **Assign macro to** a **Button F** or **Keyboard** shortcut **G** (optional).

7. Click the **OK** button to begin recording.

CONTINUE

8. The cursor changes from a mouse pointer to a "cassette" symbol to indicate *Record Mode*. Word records both the keystrokes and the commands you choose from the ribbon.

   Note: You must use keyboard commands to move the cursor or select text in Record Mode. The mouse only clicks on commands and options. See Appendix B for Keyboard Shortcuts.

9. To stop recording actions, click **Stop Recording H** on the **Macros** button dropdown menu located in the **Macros** group on the **View** tab, or click the stop button **I** on the task bar at the bottom left corner of the screen.

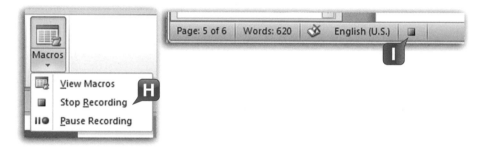

Run a Macro

1. On the **View** tab, in the **Macros** group, click **Macros**.

2. Click **View Macros**.

3. Click **Run**.

   Note: If you assigned the macro a shortcut when it was created, the macro can be run from the Quick Access Toolbar or the assigned keyboard shortcut.

 Bright Idea: There are additional macro options available through the **Developer** tab in the **Code** group. To activate the **Developer** tab, click the **File** tab and select **Options**. Select the **Developer Tab** checkbox. In the **Customize Ribbon** tab. Click **OK**.

 Option: You can also use the macro controls on the left side of the task bar to start and stop your recording session.

start   stop

48 | Apply Password Security to a Document

Difficulty: ●●○○

PROBLEM You have created a report that needs to be sent to a Review Committee. Many of the committee members have assistants with access to their mailboxes, but you only want the confidential report to be viewed or changed by the members themselves.

SOLUTION You can assign a password and activate other security options so that only those with appropriate permissions can open the document. When you password-protect a document, Word encrypts it. This password protection does not just stop the file from being opened without a password, but it physically changes the file. When you password-protect the file against changes, it simply prevents the file from being saved, unless the user has the password. For maximum security, set both passwords.

 What Microsoft Calls It: Protect Document

Step-by-Step

---

Prevent Unauthorized Readers from Opening a Document

1. Open the document you want to protect, then click the **File** tab.

2. Select **Save As**.

3. In the **Save As** dialog box, click the **Tools** button **A** in the lower left corner.

4. Choose **General Options** **B** to open the **General Options** dialog box. **Y**

5. In the **General Options** dialog box, select and type a password to open document **C**.

6. In the **Password to Modify** box, type a different password **D**. The **Password to Modify** creates a second level of protection such that you can ask for a password first to view the document, and then

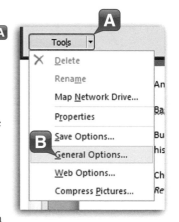

for a second password to gain permission to make changes in the document. If a viewer does not have the **Password to Modify** they will be able to read the document but not make changes.

Note: You can use one or both passwords, but if you use both, they cannot be the same password.

7. Click **OK** .

8. Confirm password(s) by re-typing it/them when prompted.

9. Click **OK** to return to the **Save As** dialog box.

10. Click **Save** to save the file with the password(s).

Step-by-Step

Change or Remove the Password Protection

1. Click the **File** tab.

2. Click **Open** and browse to find the password-protected file.

3. Click **Open**.

4. Type the password in the **Password** dialog box **F**.

5. Click **OK** **G**.

6. If prompted, type another password, and click **OK**.

7. Click the **File** tab and select **Save As**.

8. In the **Save As** dialog box, click **Tools**.

9. Choose **General Options**.

10. In the **General Options** dialog box, select and type a new password or delete the password so the password text boxes are empty.

11. Click **OK** to apply changes.

12. Click **Save** and then **Yes** to replace existing document.

Step-by-Step

Restrict Formatting and Editing

1. Open the document you want to protect.

2. On the **Review** tab, in the **Protect** group, click **Restrict Editing**  to open the **Restrict Formatting and Editing** pane on the right side of your document pane.

3. In the **Restrict Formatting and Editing** pane, apply restrictions to the following sections:
   - **Formatting restrictions:** Check this to limit the ways reviewers can make formatting changes to the document. You can also restrict them from choosing new themes and styles. Click the **Settings** link  to open the **Formatting Restrictions** dialog box and customize restrictions.
   - **Editing restrictions:** Check this to pick and choose from a variety of editing options such as comments and tracked changes. You can also limit reviewers to editing selected portions of the document.
   - **Start enforcement:** Use this section to apply the restrictions defined in the other two sections. ⚠

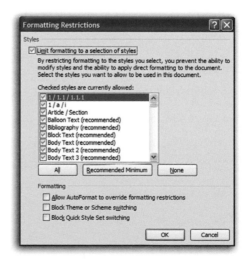

Quickest Click: You can **Encrypt with a Password** and **Restrict Editing** from the **Permissions** menu on the **Info** tab on the **File** tab.

Caution: It is critical that you remember the password, as there is no way to retrieve the password if you forget it. This means that once protected, you cannot access the file without the password.

Bright Idea: You can password protect templates to keep those filling out your forms from making changes beyond the designated fields. If your computer is secure, you might consider keeping your copy protection-free and password protecting a second copy for distribution.

Hot Tip: For better security, a password should combine lowercase and uppercase letters, along with numbers and symbols.

Caution: If you do not password protect your document, users can still make changes to these formatting and editing restrictions by opening this window.

49 | Add, Respond to, and Delete Reviewer Comments

Difficulty: ●●○○

PROBLEM You have created a document and sent it to your coworkers for review. There are several sections of the document where you want your readers to make comments and/or respond to comments. It would be easiest if the comments were incorporated into the document itself instead of in a separate document or e-mail.

SOLUTION Comments in Word are like posting little notes onto the document. A document reviewer might insert a comment to ask the author a question or make a suggestion about a specific line of text. Word tracks which reviewer made which comment, allowing you to easily follow up on a comment, get more details, or provide a response to that particular reviewer.

See Also: Monitor, Accept, and Reject Edits to a Document

 What Microsoft Calls It: Document Comments

 Step-by-Step

Create a Comment

1. Select the text you want to comment on, or place the cursor at the position in the document where the comment should be inserted.

2. On the **Review** tab, in the **Comments** group, select **New Comment A**.

3. Type your comment in the balloon and then click outside the balloon to save it.

Step-by-Step

Reading or Editing Comments

Before you can read or review comments, you need to display them on the screen.

1. On the **Review** tab, click the **Show Markup** button **B** and make sure the **Comments** option **C** is checked.

2. Click through comments, using the **Previous** and **Next** buttons **D**.

3. To edit comments, click inside the comment **E**, make your changes, and then click outside the balloon to save it.

Joseph and the Turtle

Once upon a time there was a boy who loved animals. He walked by the local pet shop every morning on his way to school. One morning while he was walking by, he noticed a new animal in the window. It was a turtle larger than the size of his head. He was amazed by what he saw. He stood in the window for a few minutes just watching the turtle. He said to himself, "I think he looks like a nice animal. I think I will stop and see him on my way home from school." And that is exactly what he did.

Comment [BB1]: What kind of turtle is this?

Comment [BB2]: Add more detail.

CONTINUE

Step-by-Step

Respond to a Comment

1. Click inside the comment balloon.

2. On the **Review** tab, in the **Comments** group, select **New Comment** .

3. Type your response in the new comment balloon and then click outside the balloon to save it. Your reply will split from the main comment line. 🔥

Step-by-Step

Delete a Comment

1. Right-click the comment indicator in the text, or inside the comment bubble.

2. Select **Delete Comment** G from the fly-out menu, or click the **Delete Comment** button H, in the **Comments** group, on the **Review** tab.

3. To delete all comments in a document, click the down arrow on the **Delete** combo button in the **Comments** group on the **Review** tab and choose **Delete All Comments in Document** I from the dropdown.

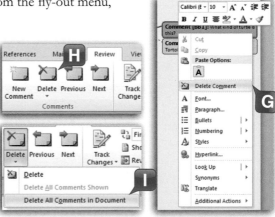

Hot Tip: Word will automatically move excess comments from the margin to the **Reviewing Pane**. The reviewing pane can sit on the side margin or bottom of the page. To use the reviewing pane to review comments, click the **Reviewing Pane** dropdown arrow  on the **Review** tab. Click **Reviewing Pane Vertical** (for display on the side of the page) or **Reviewing Pane Horizontal** (for display at bottom of the page).

50 Monitor, Accept, and Reject Edits to a Document

Difficulty: ●●○○○

PROBLEM You created a report outlining the company's strategic priorities for the upcoming year. It included product, financial, and operational information. You sent it to the marketing director, the chief financial officer, and the V.P. of operations, as well as the head of Human Resources for review and comments. You enabled the track changes feature in the document and asked each to simply mark up the page and send it back to you. Now, you need to compile the information by either accepting or rejecting the edits.

SOLUTION The process of monitoring these edits starts by setting options before sending it out for review. When multiple people edit a document, it can be unclear who suggested what changes. This can be confusing. In order to track such data, Word provides several tools that enable users to mark up a document without permanently changing the original. This provides you the ability to monitor and accept or reject those recommended changes.

See Also: Add, Respond to, and Delete Reviewer Comments

 **What Microsoft Calls It:** Track Changes

Step-by-Step

Set Track Changes Options

The Word default **Track Changes** options are useful for the basic user. However, to further customize these options for smarter editing, follow these steps:

1. On the **Review** tab, in the **Tracking** group, select **Track Changes A**.

2. Select **Change Tracking Options Options** to open the **Track Changes Options** dialog box **B**.

3. Specify the markup options you want when you make changes:

- **Insertions**: Marks inserted text.

- **Deletions**: Marks deleted text.

- **Changed Lines**: Sets the location of vertical line that marks changed paragraphs.

- **Comments Color**: Sets the color applied to all comments.

- **Formatting**: Marks formatting changes.

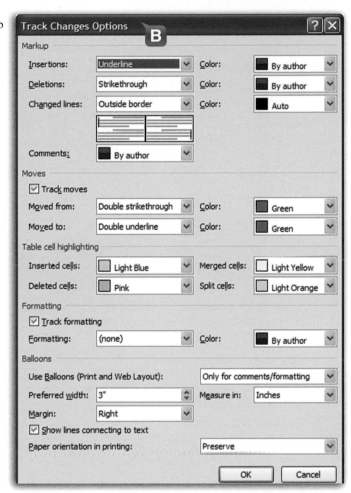

CONTINUE

4. Specify the balloon options you want to use.

   • **Use Balloons (Print and Web Layout)**: Sets display option for balloons.

   • **Preferred Width**: Sets balloon width.

   • **Margin**: Sets margin location for balloons.

5. Click **OK** to apply any changes. 🔥

Step-by-Step

Track, Accept and/or Reject Changes

1. On the **Review** tab in the **Tracking** group, select **Track Changes**.

2. After reviews are complete, respond to the review marks by either accepting or rejecting each change individually or by accepting or rejecting all changes.

3. To accept changes, select **Accept** .

4. Select either **Accept and Move to Next** or **Accept All Changes in Document**.

5. To reject changes, select **Reject** **D**.

6. Select either **Reject and Move to Next** or **Reject All Changes in Document**.

Hot Tip: If you specify any of the colors in the dialog box as *By author,* Word will automatically assign a different color to each person's changes and comments. Word determines if a new person is editing the document by looking at the User Name set up in Word. This is especially useful when you have multiple editors.

51 | Identify the Difference between Two Documents

Difficulty: ●●●●

PROBLEM You are working on a project with your coworkers. You send out a draft for everyone to review and provide feedback. Each of your coworkers, one at a time, begins sending their versions back to you. You have to incorporate everyone's suggestions and changes into a master document.

SOLUTION If you want to compare multiple versions of a document and create one master copy, you can compare and merge these documents using Word 2010. The changes can be automatically merged into one document or viewed for comparison. When you compare or merge documents, the text that differs between the two versions will be highlighted in a different color or with tracking marks.

 What Microsoft Calls It: Compare and Combine Documents

Step-by-Step

Viewing Two Documents Side by Side

1. Open both documents.

2. Display one of the two as the active document.

3. On the **View** tab, in the **Window** group, click **View Side by Side** .

   Note: If only two documents are open, Word will automatically place them side by side. If more than two are open, the Compare Side by Side dialog box **B** *opens. The main document will be active. Select the document to compare to and click OK.*

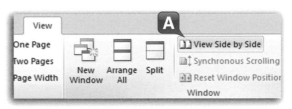

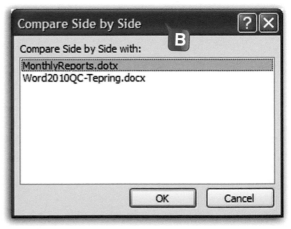

4. The two windows are set for synchronized scrolling, allowing you to compare the documents line by line.

   Note: To turn off synchronized scrolling, click the Synchronous Scrolling button  *in the Window group on the View tab.*

**Step-by-Step**

Comparing and Combining Documents

Combine merges the revisions from both copies into a single document, which can be either the original or the copy, as you specify, or a brand-new document. You can repeat the combine operation to combine revisions from multiple copies. All unique revision marks are kept in both copies.

Compare generates a new copy that combines the two versions, and the revision marks are now combined and not attributable to specific reviewers.

1. On the **Review** tab, in the **Compare** group, click **Compare D**.

2. Click **Combine** from the menu **E**.

3. In the **Combine Documents** dialog box, select or browse to the original document from the **Original document** dropdown menu **F**.

4. Open the **Revised document** dropdown menu **G** and select the other document to combine.

5. By default, the **Label unmarked changes with** setting is whatever user name is set up in Word as the current user. This can be edited.

6. Click the **More** button  to set additional options:

- **Comparison settings:** Clear the check boxes for any comparisons you want to omit.

- **Show changes at:** By default, revisions are marked at the Word level, but you can set this to Character level if you prefer.

- **Show changes in:** Choose where the combined markup will appear. You can choose to place the revisions in the **Original document**, the **Revised document**, or a new document.

7. Click **OK** to combine the documents.

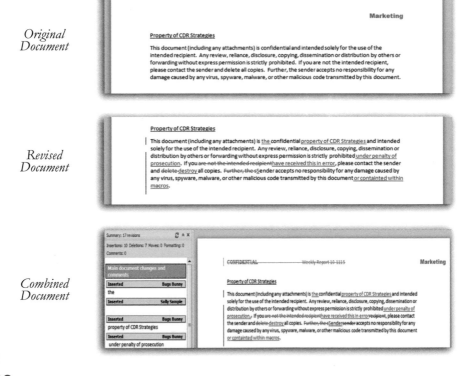

Original Document

Revised Document

Combined Document

Hot Tip: Compare multiple versions in the same Word window. From your combined document, click **Compare** D on the **Review** tab, in the **Compare** group, and then click **Show Source Documents** I. Check **Show Both** J from the fly-out menu. Your windows editing pane will split to display the **Combined document** K, the **Original document** L and the **Revised document** M within the same window. In the example, the **Reviewing Pane** N is also active.

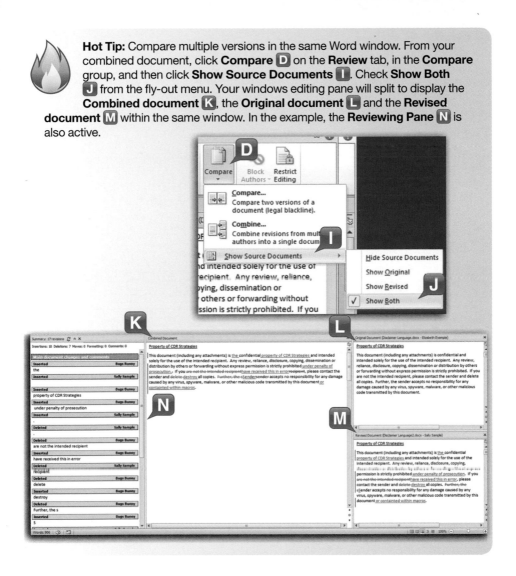

Identify the Difference between Two Documents   **187**

52 | Import Data from an Excel Spreadsheet into a Document

Difficulty: ●●○○

PROBLEM You maintain a customer contact list in Excel. You are currently producing a memo to go out to all regional managers. The memo includes a variety of information—all text. You want to include the data from Excel in the spreadsheet without having to recreate the table.

SOLUTION Import the data from Excel and then format and sort it right in your Word document.

 What Microsoft Calls It: Insert Object

Step-by-Step

1. Place the cursor in the position where the Excel spreadsheet will be inserted.

2. On the **Insert** tab in the **Text** group, select **Object** **A** to open the **Object** dialog box.

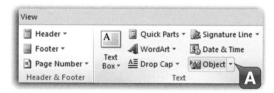

3. On the **Create From File** tab **B**, click **Browse** **C** to locate and select the file to include in the document.

4. Click **OK** **D**.

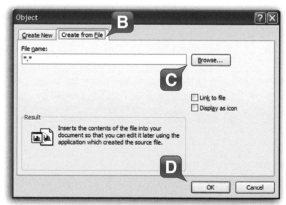

Alliance Coffee Company, Inc.

Sales Rep	Region	First Name	Last Name
Jones	NE	Sandy	Gayle
Jones	NE	Peter	Grandy
Sandoval	SW	Ken	Killbrew
Baker	SW	Samuel	Elsworth
Kasar	W	Jack	Morton
Kasar	W	Harry	Hickes
Kasar	W	Elizabeth	Cramden
Kasar	W	Gina	Gamerly
Kasar	W	Fred	Newell
Kasar	W	Harry	Hickes
Kasar	NW	Frank	Filbert
Kasar	NW	Gina	Gamerly
Kasar	NW	Fred	Newell
Kasar	NW	Joel	Austerman
Kasar	NW	Frank	Filbert
Kasar	NW	Sandy	Galye
Kasar	NW	Mort	Ellery
Kasar	NW	Xavier	Kherr
Silver	NE	Jamie	Jeremiah
Silver	SE	Richard	Huckabe

Bright Idea: You can insert a blank Excel spreadsheet into an existing word document. This allows for data manipulation that a Word table does not allow, such as flexibility in sorting, formatting, and formulas/functions. On the **Insert** tab in the **Text** group, select **Object**. In the **Create New** tab, select an Excel spreadsheet in the format you desire. Click **OK**.

Double-click any Excel spreadsheet object to edit its contents.

STOP

53

Use Data from an Excel Spreadsheet to Populate Fields in a Document

Difficulty: ●●○○

PROBLEM You have a donor list created in Excel that contains all donors' names, home addresses and giving amounts. You are getting ready to send out a brochure advertising the Appreciation Banquet and you want to personalize each letter without typing in every name and address into your form letter.

SOLUTION Use Mail Merge to create your letters, envelopes, and RSVP forms.

Mail Merge is a tool in Microsoft Word that allows you to merge a list of data stored in a data source (an Excel spreadsheet, an Access database, a comma-separated value text file, etc.) with fields in a Word document.

There are several benefits to using a mail merge to create your documents:

- The process can save you a great deal of time and effort.
- Data can be stored one place and sent to you in a single ready-to-use file.
- Errors are reduced, as you are not retyping information already entered.
- Personalized communication tends to yield better results than form letters.

> **What Microsoft Calls It:** Mail Merge

Step-by-Step

Create a Mail Merge with a Microsoft Word Document

1. Configure your Excel spreadsheet so that all data to be used in the merge is in columns.

2. Make sure that each column header contains only alphanumeric characters and spaces. Words may be separated by an underscore , but no other punctuation characters should be used.

	A	B	C	D	E
1	Donor_Level	Honorific	Donor	Donation	Donation Date
2	Bronze	Mrs.	Gayle	$ 25.00	1/1/2011
3	Master	Mr.	Morton	$ 954.00	1/1/2011
4	Honor	Dr. and Mrs.	Elsworth	$ 8,846.00	1/1/2011
5	Bronze	Professor	Grandy	$ 13,485.00	1/1/2011
6	Silver	Ms.	Jeremiah	$ 34,075.00	1/1/2011
7	Silver	Mr. and Dr.	Huckabe	$ 45,387.00	1/1/2011
8	Gold	Mr. and Mrs.	Killbrew	$ 87,934.00	1/1/2011

3. Save the workbook.

4. In Microsoft Word, prepare the document into which you intend to insert the merge data.

5. Click the **Start Mail Merge** dropdown button **B** in the **Start Mail Merge** group of the **Mailings** tab.

6. Select **Step by Step Mail Merge Wizard** **C**. The **Mail Merge** task pane will open beside your document.

7. In **Step 1** of the wizard, select what type of document you want to create **D**, then click the **Next: Starting document** **E** link at the bottom of the **Mail Merge** task pane.

8. In **Step 2** of the wizard, you will select your starting document and make layout decisions based on what kind of document you are creating. These options will change based upon the type of document you selected in Step 1. Click the **Next: Select recipients** link at the bottom of the **Mail Merge** task pane.

9. In **Step 3** of the wizard, select the data source worksheet by clicking the **Browse** option **F** under the **Use an existing list** heading.

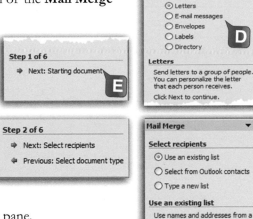

CONTINUE

10. Browse to the workbook and click **Open** to launch the **Select Table** dialog box.

11. Select the appropriate sheet within the workbook **G** and click **OK** to launch the **Mail Merge Recipients** **H** dialog box. From this window, you can sort data by columns and filter, add, or remove recipients from your merge.

12. When your recipients list is ready, click **OK**.

13. In **Step 4** of the wizard, position your cursor where you would like to insert a merge field in the document.

14. Click the **More Items** option **I** in the **Mail Merge** task panel.

15. Select the field you want to insert **J** in the **Fields** window.

16. Click the **Insert** button **K**.

17. Repeat steps 13 through 16 as often as necessary to insert all required merge fields **L**.

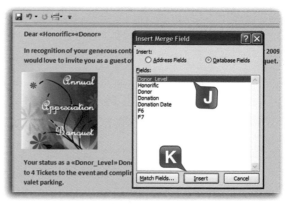

Dear «Honorific»«Donor»

In recognition of your generous contributions to our organization in the fiscal year 2009-2010, would love to invite you as a guest of honor to the 2011 Annual Appreciation Banquet.

Your status as a «Donor_Level» Donor entitles you to 4 Tickets to the event and complimentary valet parking.

18. Click the **Next: Preview your letters** link ⓜ.

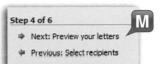

Step 4 of 6 ⓜ
➡ Next: Preview your letters
◄ Previous: Select recipients

19. Review the data in the merge fields ⓝ.

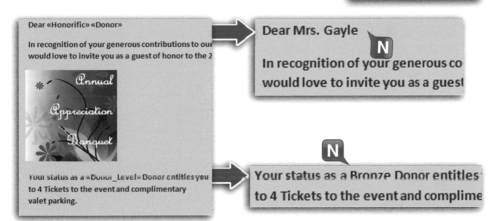

20. Click the **Next: Complete the merge** link ⓞ.

Step 5 of 6 ⓞ
➡ Next: Complete the merge
◄ Previous: Write your letter

21. Your merge is ready to produce your letters. In **Step 6**, you can print your documents with the merged information imbedded, or you can edit them individually.

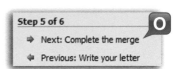

CONTINUE

- To print, click the **Print** link 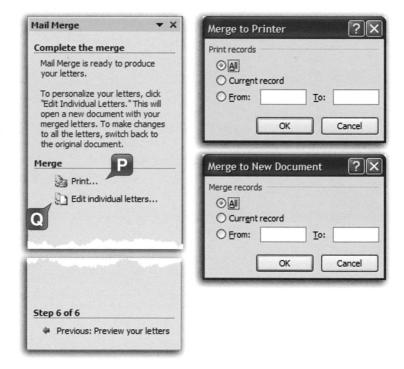 **P** under the **Merge** heading in the **Mail Merge** task panel. This will open the **Merge to Printer** dialog box where you can choose to print **All** the merged records, the **Current record**, or a range of records. Click **OK** to launch your printer's **Print** dialog box.

- To view or edit each letter individually, click the **Edit individual letters** link **Q**. This will open the **Merge to New Document** dialog box where you can choose to view print **All** the merged records, the **Current record,** or a range of records. Click **OK**. Your letters will be compiled into a single file with a page break between each copy of the letter.

Bright Idea: You can create merge fields in any document. In addition to address labels and envelopes, this feature can be used to produce certificates, personalized letters, invitations, product labels, name tags, seating cards, advertising flyers, marketing collateral, retail item placards, newsletters – you name it!

 Quickest Click: You can set up your main document manually, create, or open a document. Click the Start Mail Merge button **R** on the Mailings tab. Select the type of document you want to merge, then select your options when prompted.

 Quickest Click: You can connect your document to a data source manually. Click the Select Recipients button **S** on the Mailings tab, then select the type of data source you want to merge. Make option selections when prompted.

54 | Create a PowerPoint Presentation from a Word Document

Difficulty: ●●●○

PROBLEM The head of the department just informed you that you need to create a PowerPoint presentation using the data from your Monthly Overview Report to present to the executive team in three hours.

SOLUTION You can create a Microsoft PowerPoint presentation from an existing Word document. The Word document should be structured like an outline, using the predesigned heading styles in Word. PowerPoint uses these heading styles in the Word document to format the titles of each slide. For example, text formatted with the Heading 1 style becomes the title of a new slide. Text formatted with Heading 2 becomes the first level of text. This process will continue for all data formatted in this manner.

See Also: Insert a Numbered or Bulleted List; Apply Styles to Text

 Step-by-Step

Create a PowerPoint Presentation

1. Create an outline of the presentation.

2. Select each slide title and format it as **Heading 1 A**.

3. Select each sub-heading and format it as **Heading 2 B**.

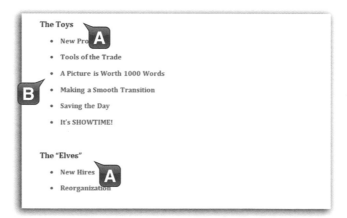

4. Save the document and close it.

5. Open **PowerPoint** and create a new presentation.

6. Add a new slide after the title slide.

7. On that new slide, click the dropdown arrow at the bottom of the **New Slide** button and select **Slides from Outline**.

8. Browse to your Word file and select it.

9. Click the **Open** button.

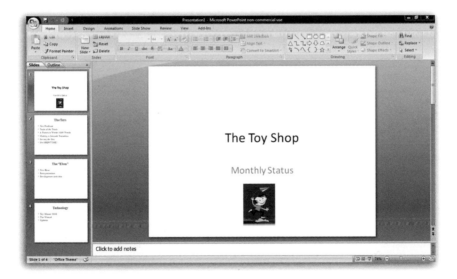

 Hot Tip: To save time formatting, decide what theme you want to use in the PowerPoint Slide Show. Use that same theme when you assign the heading styles to your outline in Word, as the selected style carries over into PowerPoint when you import the outline to the slides.

55 | Create a Form with Fillable Fields

Difficulty:

PROBLEM You want to do a widespread survey through e-mail of your customers to get updates on contact information, as well as provide customers with an opportunity to make comments on service or products.

SOLUTION You can create a form in Word to e-mail to your customer group. With fillable fields, the form can be very quick and easy for the customers to complete and return. Forms enable you to gather information using fill-in-the-blank fields. Form fields (such as text, picture, list boxes, and date pickers) are called **Content Controls** in Word 2010. Using forms in Microsoft Word is a great option for those who do not have the technical skill or platform to create web forms. Forms created in Word can be printed and completed on paper or filled out from within Word.

See Also: Perform Calculations in a Table; Create Templates; Add a Table to a Document; Format Layout; Format Table Text; Table Borders, and Shading; Apply Borders and Shading to Text or a Page; Apply Password Security to a Document

> **What Microsoft Calls It:** Content Controls, Legacy Controls, ActiveX Controls

Step-by-Step

Enable the Developer Tab

The **Developer** tab is required to create **Content Controls** in Word. If you don't see the **Developer** tab on your ribbon, you need to enable it.

1. Click the **File** tab.

2. Click the **Options** button **A** to launch the **Word Options** dialog box.

3. Click the **Customize Ribbon** tab **B**.

4. Click the **Developer** checkbox **C** so it is checked in the **Main Tabs** box.

5. Click the **OK** button. The **Developer** tab **D** will now appear on the ribbon.

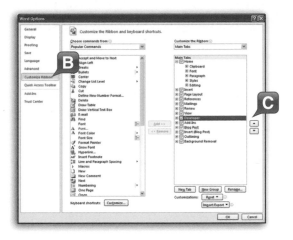

Step-by-Step

Create a Form

The first thing you need to do is design the layout of your form. Many authors elect to use tables to provide structure for the form layout. Using tables helps to line up the text, instructions, or labels for **Content Controls** in an organized manner. By using a table for the layout, you can add borders and/or shading for a more artistic presentation, or you may elect to use no borders or shading for a clean look. Or you may opt for other formatting, such as adding multiple columns to a page.

This is an individual design preference. For this example, a table was created and all text was added in preparation for inserting the **Content Controls.**

After you have finished designing the form, add the form fields—called **Content Controls**. These controls are where those filling out the form insert their information. **Content Controls**, located on the **Developer** tab in the **Controls** group, include **Text** boxes, **Images**, **Dropdown** menus, **Dates**, and **Legacy Tools**.

1. Place your cursor in the position where you want to add a form field **E**.

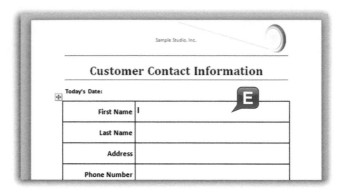

2. Hover over the graphic icons in the **Controls** group on the **Developer** tab to see the text describing each control **F**.

3. Select the control you want to insert into your form:

- **Rich Text G**: Text boxes that hold a paragraph of formatted text. This is useful where you need to fill in information. The Rich Text control allows users typing in the information to format the text within the box to their specifications. For example, they can type in their information and italicize or bold a certain word. Or they can change the color of the font on their entry.

- **Plain Text H**: Use the plain Text box for most forms. The advantage of these controls is that they can hold more than one paragraph. Rich text controls only allow one paragraph.

- **Picture I**: This control feature allows images to be inserted, such as photos, logos, charts, etc.

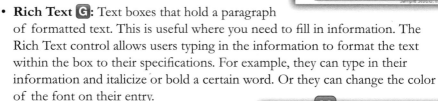

- **Combo Box J**: This control feature displays a list of options and includes a text box for entries that do not appear on the list. Use a combo box to provide "suggested" options, but still allow users to enter their own information.

- **Dropdown List K:** This provides users a dropdown menu that limits the options users can choose from. This is especially useful when you want a user to choose only one of the options, such as Yes/No, or from which city or state they reside. This also eliminates spelling errors or typos that could lead to errors.

- **Date Picker L:** This is a calendar tool that lets users easily select a date.

- **Check Box M:** This inserts a check box control that lets users toggle a check on or off.

- **Building Block Gallery N:** Building blocks are predesigned, preformatted chunks of text, pictures, and other content that people can insert into documents.

- **Legacy Tools O:** These are controls and form fields used in previous versions of Word. These do not have the same functionality as the new content controls, and are primarily used only to edit a form that was developed in a previous version of Word.   *Note: Radio buttons are only available in Legacy Tools.*

4. Your Content Control will appear in your document with the relevant prompt text **P**.

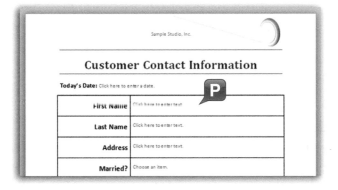

56 Set Properties for Content Controls

Difficulty: ●●○○

PROBLEM You have a form with Content Controls, but you need to edit the titles and tags and make other changes to the settings. You would also like to protect your form so that users may read and fill out the information but not be able to make changes.

SOLUTION Each Content Control has properties that you can edit to customize. Content Controls can be locked so that users cannot delete or edit the contents.

Step-by-Step

Set Properties for Content Controls

1. Click the **Design Mode** button  in the **Controls** group, on the **Developer** tab.

2. Click on an individual **Content Control** within the form to edit.

3. Right-click and select **Properties** from the menu to launch the **Content Control Properties** dialog box.

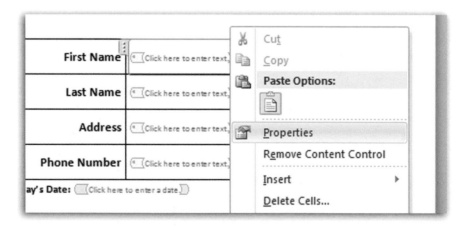

4. Under the **General** heading of the **Content Control Properties** dialog box, you can define a **Title** **B** for the content control tab and assign **Tags** **C** that are used by other computer programs to identify and then read or write the contents in your control. You can also choose and define **Style** settings **D**.

5. Under the **Locking** heading, you can set your protection preferences:

- **Content control cannot be deleted:** Check this box **E** to protect the field from being deleted by users.

- **Content control cannot be edited:** Check this box **F** to protect the control from being edited by users. This is useful if you want to display the information in the control without users being able to edit. This can be useful in other types of documents as well.

6. The last third of the **Content Control Properties** dialog box will have different property values available, based on the type of **Content Control** you are editing:

- **Allow carriage returns (multiple paragraphs):** Check this box to allow users to put several paragraphs in a Text control.

- **Remove content control when contents are edited:** Check this box to create a prompt for the document. Once a user types in text, the content control disappears and the text takes its place.

- **Dropdown List Properties:** Both the **Combo Box** and the **Dropdown** list content controls contain properties where you provide words and options for the lists.

- **Display the date like this:** This is a property field in the **Date Picker.** This is where you choose the format for the date (i.e., January 12, 2010 vs 1/12/10).

- **Locale and Calendar type:** These are property fields used in the **Date Picker.** These are used to control the way dates are shown in different regions and languages.

- **Store XML contents in the following format when mapped:** This option is used in the **Date Picker** control to communicate date information to other programs.

- **Gallery and Category:** These options are used in the **Building Block Gallery** control to select specific building blocks that can be inserted into the document.

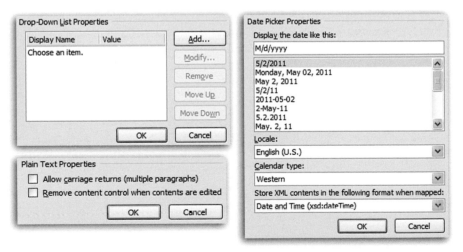

Step-by-Step

Protect Your Form

1. Click the **Restrict Editing** button 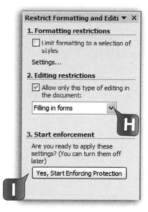, in the **Protect** group, on the **Developer** tab.

2. The **Restrictions Pane** opens on the right side of the document. Under **Editing Restrictions**, check **Allow Only** and then choose **Filling in Forms** 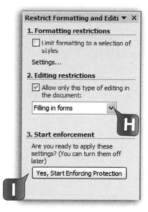.

3. Click **Yes, Start Enforcing Protection** 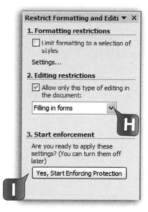.

4. You will be prompted to enter a password. You do not have to enter a password to protect the document, but without the password, users will be able to turn off the protection and modify the form.

 Caution: If you choose to enter a password, be sure to remember it, as Word cannot retrieve it.

 Hot Tip: To turn off protection, click **Restrict Editing** again, and click the **Stop Protection** button. You will be prompted for the password.

57 | Customize the Ribbon

Difficulty: ●●○○

PROBLEM You have a set of commands that you use regularly. Several of these commands are unique to your work and are buried under several clicks by default. You want a way to bring these commands within easy reach.

SOLUTION Customize the Ribbon.

Office 2010 introduced the ability to customize ribbon commands to a much greater degree. In 2010, you can create custom tabs and groups, rename and change the order of default tabs and groups, and hide both custom and default tabs.

To access the Customize options, click on the **File** tab, then click the **Options** button. This will launch the **Word Options** dialog box **A**. Click on the **Customize Ribbon** tab **B**.

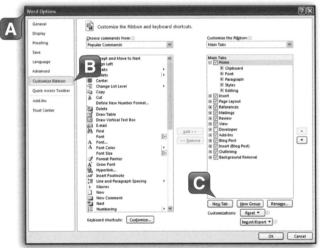

Step-by-Step

Customize Tabs

1. To add a new tab to the **Ribbon**, click the **New Tab** button **C** under the **Customize the Ribbon:** window. A new tab with the name **New Tab (Custom)** will appear in the list.

2. Right-click on the new tab and select the **Rename** menu option 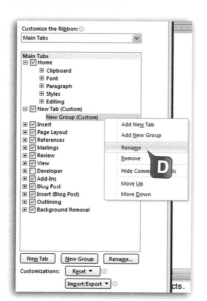. Type your custom tab name in the **Display Name** field of **Rename** dialog box 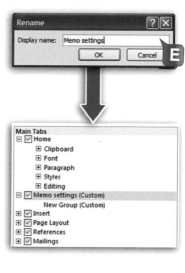.

3. Click the **OK** button.

4. To move your new tab up and down on the list (or right and left on the Ribbon), select it, then click the up/down arrows to the right of the window .

5. To hide any tab from being displayed on the ribbon, click the checkbox to the left of each tab  to uncheck it. Click again to unhide the tab and have it displayed in the Ribbon.

6. If you decide to remove a custom tab, right-click the tab in the **Customize the Ribbon** list, then select **Remove** . *Note: You can hide, but you cannot remove default tabs.*

Step-by-Step

Customize Groups

1. Click the **Expand** button **I** to the left of any tab to view the groups that appear on the tab **J**.

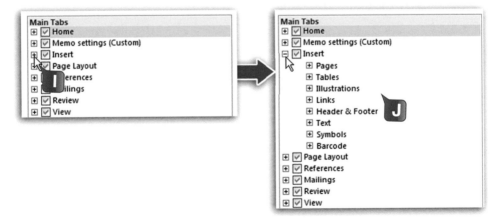

2. To add a new group to any tab, select the tab you want the group to appear on, then click the **New Group** button **K** under the **Customize the Ribbon:** window. A new group with the name **New Group (Custom)** will appear in the list.

3. Right-click on the new group and select the **Rename** menu option .Type your custom group name in the **Display name** field of the **Rename** dialog box . You can also select an icon to represent your custom group by clicking on any image in the **Symbol** selection box **N**.

4. Click the **OK** button.

5. To move your new group up and down on the list (or right and left on the tab), select it, then click the up/down arrows to the right of the **Customize the Ribbon** list.

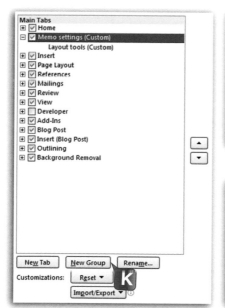

6. If you decide to remove any group from a tab, right-click the group in the **Customize the Ribbon** list, then select **Remove** – OR – select the group, then click the **Remove** button 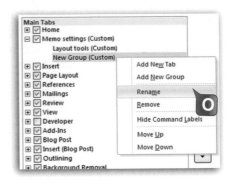 between the **Choose** and **Customize** windows.

Step-by-Step

Add Commands to a Custom Group

1. Commands can only be added to custom groups, so begin by following the steps in the *Customize Groups* section to create a group for your commands.

2. Click on the command you want to add **P** in the **Choose commands from** window.

3. Select the custom group as the destination **Q**.

4. Click the **Add** button **R**. Repeat as needed.

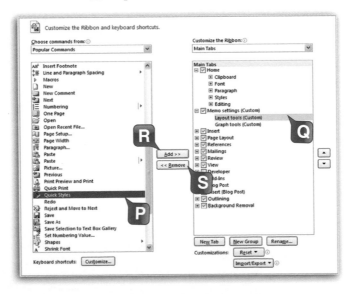

5. The command will appear under your custom group in the **Customize the Ribbon** list.

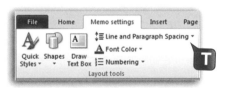

6. To rename a command that you have added to a custom group, right-click on the command and select the **Rename** menu option **L**. Type your command name in the **Rename** dialog box **M**. You can also select an icon to represent your custom group by clicking on any image in the **Symbol:** selection box **N**.

7. To move a command up and down on the list, select it, then click the up/down arrows to the right of the window **F**.

8. If you decide to remove a command from your custom group, right-click the group in the **Customize the Ribbon:** list, then select **Remove – OR –** select the group, then click the **Remove** button **S** between the **Choose** and **Customize** windows. *Note: You cannot remove commands from default groups, although you **can** remove entire groups from tabs.*

9. When you have made all your changes, click **OK** in the **Word Options** dialog box to save your settings and return to your document. Review your customized tab **T**.

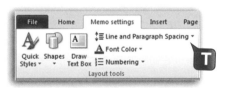

Quickest Click: Right-click any item in the **Customize the Ribbon:** window for shortcuts to add new tabs or groups, show or hide tabs, and move tabs up or down.

58 | Define Shortcut Keys

Difficulty: ●●○○

PROBLEM Every week you transcribe your notes from the departmental meeting into a memo to share with your supervisors. You are fast and efficient when you can keep your hands on the keyboard, but the memo's style requires a few formatting commands that do not have Word shortcut keys assigned to them. You would like a way to activate those commands without moving your hand to the mouse.

SOLUTION Customize keyboard shortcuts so you can perform your favorite commands by using quick keyboard strokes.

Step-by-Step

Define a Keyboard Shortcut

1. To access the **Customize** options, click on the **File** tab, then click the **Options** button **A**. This will launch the **Word Options** dialog box. Click on the **Customize Ribbon** tab **B**.

2. Click the **Customize** button **C** in the **Customize the Ribbon and keyboard shortcuts** pane to open the **Customize Keyboard** dialog box.

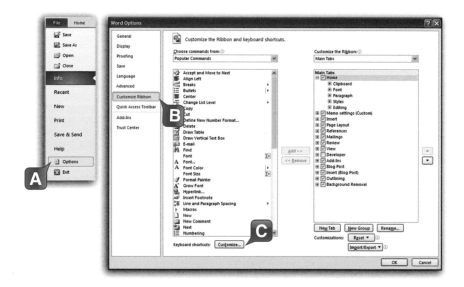

3. In the **Categories**: box **D**, select the name of the tab that contains the command for which you want a shortcut. If you don't know the tab, or can't find the command under a tab, select **All Commands** or **Commands not in the Ribbon**.

4. In the **Commands** box **E**, select the command you want a shortcut for.

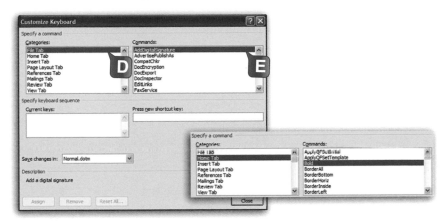

5. Any shortcuts already assigned to the command will appear in the **Current keys** box **F**. Click in the **Press new shortcut key** box **G**, then type the combination of keys you want to assign to that command. Keyboard shortcuts must begin with **CTRL** or a function key.

   *Note: If you make a mistake in selecting your shortcut, use the **Backspace** key on your keyboard to remove it. The **Delete** key is considered one of the keystrokes. If you hit the **Delete** key, "Del" appears in the text box.*

6. Look at **Currently assigned to:** **H** to make sure the combination you have chosen is not already assigned to another command. ⚠

In the **Save changes in** dropdown , choose the document or template that you want the shortcut changes to apply to. If you select the current document, the keyboard shortcut will only work when you are editing that document. If you select Normal.dotm, the changes will be made to the default Word template and all new documents will contain the shortcut (unless you are working from another custom template).

7. Click **Assign** .

Caution: If you reassign a combination of keys, you will no longer be able to use the combination for its original purpose. For example, if you reassign **CTRL+B** (bold) to the **BulletsGallery** command, you will not be able make text bold by typing **CTRL+B**.

Hot Tip: To remove a keyboard shortcut so it will not activate a specific command, click the shortcut you want to remove in the **Current keys** box , then click **Remove** . If you want to remove all custom shortcuts and return your template/document to Word's defaults, click **Reset All** .

Bright Idea: You can also create keyboard shortcuts to activate Macros, Fonts, Building Blocks, Styles, and Common Symbols for even more efficiency.

59 Sending Documents from Word

Difficulty: ●●○○

PROBLEM You regularly create documents that you distribute to your department via email attachments. You would like a faster way to do this this once each one is completed and save steps in clicking through file folders each time you attach the file.

SOLUTION Use the **Send Using E-mail** options in the **Save & Send** tab of the Backstage view to e-mail documents directly from Word. *Note: This tip only applies if you use Microsoft Outlook as your default e-mail client.*

Step-by-Step

Send Using E-mail

1. Click on the **File** tab, then click on the **Save & Send** tab **A** in the Backstage view. Make sure the **Send Using E-mail** sub-tab **B** is selected.

2. Choose how you want your document to be distributed by making a selection in the **Send Using E-mail** menu **C**.

- **Send as Attachment** – A copy of your document in its original file format **D** will be attached to an e-mail message.

  If there are multiple recipients, each will receive a separate copy. Changes made in these copies will not be reflected in the original or in the other

  copies. You will have to manually consolidate any changes and feedback from recipients into your original.

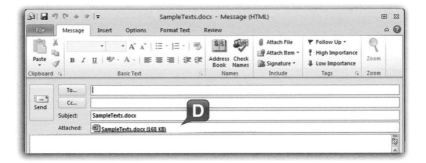

- **Send a Link** – An e-mail message will be opened that contains a URL link  to the document.

  NOTE: This is only available if the document is saved in a shared location such as Windows Live SkyDrive. You will receive a warning and this option will be unavailable if your document is not saved to a shared location.

- **Send as PDF** – A copy of your document will be converted to PDF format and attached to an e-mail message.

  PDF format is useful because it looks the same on most computers, allowing you to control exactly what the recipient will see and print, including fonts, formatting and images. Recipients will not be able to change your original data, but they will be able to view your document, even if they do not have Word installed on their machine. NOTE: Your recipients will have to have a PDF reader installed on their computers to view the document. Readers such as **Adobe's Acrobat Reader** are free and easily available.⚠

- **Send as XPS** – A copy of your document will be converted to XPS format and attached to an e-mail message.

  The XPS format offers many of the same benefits as PDF, in addition to embedded fonts and more precise image and color rendering.

Caution: When you click **Send as PDF**, the default **Save As PDF (*.pdf)** setting will be used. Make sure you are satisfied with the results before you send your e-mail. If you don't like the way the PDF looks, make changes in the **Page Setup** group on the **Page Layout** tab and review in the **Print Preview** panel before clicking **Send as PDF** again.

If you wish to e-mail a PDF or XPS of only certain pages within the document (or change other settings), click the **Create PDF/XPS Document** tab **F** in the **Save & Send** panel. Open the **Publish as PDF or XPS** dialog box. Select **PDF (*.pdf)** in the **Save as type** dropdown **G**, then click the **Options** **H** button to launch the **Options** dialog box **I** and choose the settings you want for your PDF.

60 Save Your Document to Windows Live SkyDrive

Difficulty: ●●●●

PROBLEM You frequently use several different computers – your desktop in the office, your laptop at home, and client workstations when you are traveling. You would like an easier way to update and view your documents without having to constantly copy them to thumb drives or e-mail them from one machine to another.

SOLUTION Save your documents to Windows Live SkyDrive.

With a Windows Live account, your SkyDrive acts as an external file folder that you can access via any machine with Internet access. Changes you make will be available on any computer the next time you log in and work on the document.

Step-by-Step

Save Your Document to Windows Live SkyDrive

1. When your document is ready to share, go to the **File** tab, then click on the **Save & Send** tab  in the **Backstage** view.

2. Click **Save to Web** sub-tab **B** in the **Save & Send** pane.

3. If you have a Windows Live ID (or Hotmail, Windows Messenger, or XBOX Live ID), click the **Sign In** button **C**

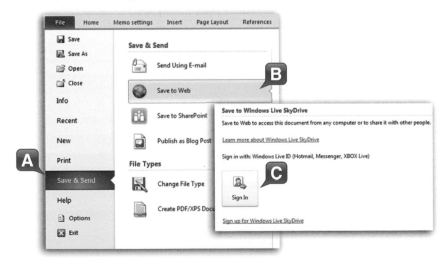

Hot Tip: If you need to create an ID, click **Sign up for Windows Live SkyDrive**  **D**. Your default Web browser will launch to the Windows live login site. Click the **Sign up** button **E** and follow the directions to create an account.

4. Enter your account's E-mail address in the **E-mail address** text box **F** and your Windows Live password in the **Password** text box **G** in the **Connecting to docs.live.net** dialog box. Click **OK**.

5. In the **Backstage** view, your **Save to Windows Live SkyDrive** pane will change to show your account name **H** and SkyDrive folders **I**. Click on the folder you want your document saved into, then click **Save As** button **J**.

CONTINUE

6. In the **Save As** dialog box, type in the name you want to give your document in the **File name** text box **K**. Click the **Save** button. Your document is now saved on your Windows Live SkyDrive.

Step-by-Step

Opening a document from SkyDrive

1. When you are ready to open a document from your SkyDrive, go to the **File** tab, then click the **Open** button **A** in the **Backstage** view.

2. Click **Save to Web** sub-tab **B** in the **Save & Send** pane.

3. Click the **Sign In** button and log in to Windows Live.

4. When your **Save to Windows Live SkyDrive** pane has updated to show your account name **H** and SkyDrive folders **I**, click on the **Open** tab **J** in the **File** menu.

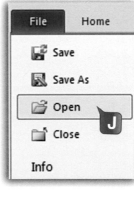

5. In the **Open** dialog box 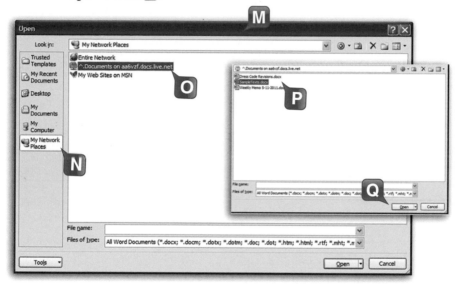 click on the **My Network Places** button **N**. Now that you are logged in to Windows Live, you will see your SkyDrive folders under the **My Network Places** dropdown. Double click the SkyDrive folder that contains your document **O**, then select the document you wish to open **P**.

6. Click the **Open** button **Q**.

61 | Create a New Folder On Windows Live SkyDrive

Difficulty: ●●●●

PROBLEM You have several documents that you keep on your SkyDrive for easy access from different computers. You would like to organize your files by project so you can find them more quickly and keep track of versions more easily.

SOLUTION Create folders and sub-folders to organize your files.

Just like on your local hard drive, you can create folders and sub-folders on your Windows Live SkyDrive. Since all files and folders are accessed through a Web browser, it is somewhat more difficult to create and organize folders on your SkyDrive. Once you become comfortable with the SkyDrive user interface, however, you will be able to organize your files for quick reference and sharing.

 Step-by-Step

Create a new folder on your SkyDrive from Word

1. When you are ready to open a document from your SkyDrive, go to the **File** tab, then click on the **Save & Send** tab **A** in the **Backstage** view.

2. Click **Save to Web** sub-tab **B** in the **Save & Send** pane.

3. Click the **Sign In** button **C** and log in to Windows Live.

4. When your **Save to Windows Live SkyDrive** pane has updated to show your account name **D** and SkyDrive folders **E**, click on the **Windows Live SkyDrive** link **F** above the **Personal Folders** heading. This will launch your default Web browser and open a window to your Windows Live folders.

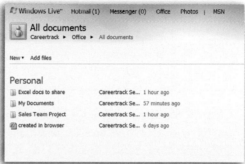

5. In the **New** dropdown **G** select **Folder** **H**. If you wish to create a sub-folder, browse to another folder first, then click **New**.

6. On the **Create a folder** dialog page, replace **New Folder** with your title in the **Name** text box **I**.

7. Click **Next** **J**.

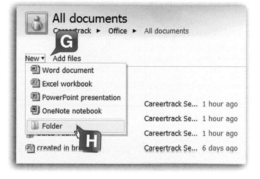

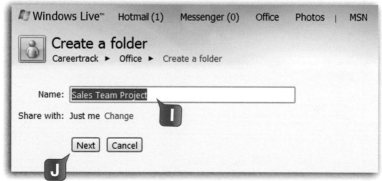

CONTINUE

8. Your folder will be created and you will be taken to the file view for your new folder with a prompt to add content **K**.

9. Click the **SkyDrive** option **L** in the **Windows Live** dropdown **M** located in the top left corner of your browser window to view your new SkyDrive folder **N** and create more folders or sub-folders if you wish.

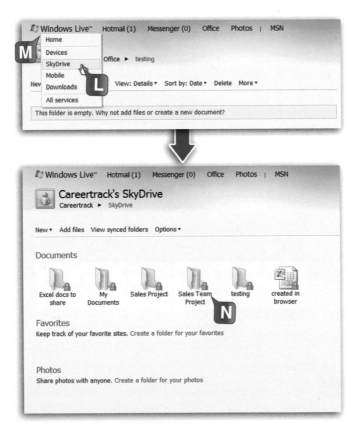

10. To save documents into your new folder(s), return to Word 2010, open the file you wish to put into your new folder then return to the **Save to Web** sub-tab under **Save & Send** in the **File** menu. To see your new folder(s)  **O** in the **Save to Windows Live SkyDrive** panel, click the **Refresh** button **P**.

11. Click **Save As** button **Q**.

62

Share Your Document Using Windows Live SkyDrive

Difficulty: ●●●●

PROBLEM You have a document that several people need to review and edit. You usually send the data to your colleagues through e-mail, but then you spend hours updating the changes into your original spreadsheet. Sometimes it's hard to tell what changes were made recently. You would like an easier way to collaborate.

SOLUTION Share the document on Windows Live.

With a Windows Live account, your SkyDrive acts as an external file folder that you can invite others to access. All changes are made directly into the original. *Note: You must have Internet access and a Windows Live account to complete this tip.*

Step-by-Step

Share Your Document

1. Go to the **File** tab, then click on the **Save & Send** tab **A** in the **Backstage** view.

2. Click **Save to Web** sub-tab **B** in the **Save & Send** pane.

3. Click on the **Windows Live SkyDrive** link **C** in the **Save to Windows Live SkyDrive** pane. This will launch your default Web browser and open a window to your Windows Live folders.

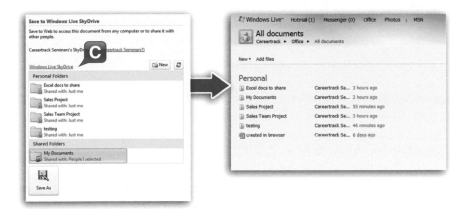

4. Browse to, then hover over, the name of the top-level folder that contains the files you wish to share. A popup menu will appear.

5. Click on the **Share** link, then select **Edit Permissions** from the dropdown **D**.

6. In the **Edit Permissions** window, choose the level of sharing you want by sliding the selection arrow **E** to the setting you want.

- **Me:** The folder is private. Only you, and people you add individually via e-mail address, can view and edit the contents.

- **Some friends:** You define a limited set of people who can access the files. These can consist of people chosen from your Windows Live social network ("friends"), or from your contacts list.

- **Friends:** All of your Windows Live social network "friends" will have access to the folder.

CONTINUE

- **My friends and their friends:** All of your Windows Live social network "friends" AND their friends will have access to the files.

- **Everyone (public):** Everyone can see the files.

7. Define the control level settings for each level of sharing by choosing one of the options from the pulldown menus 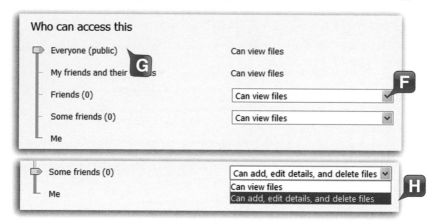.

   - **Can view files:** People with access to the files will be able to read and download the files, but they can not change the files or upload new ones to the folder. This is the default choice. This is the only choice available for the **My friends and their friends** and **Everyone (public)** setting **G**.

   - **Can add, edit details, and delete files:** People with access to the files will be allowed to make changes to the files, upload new files, and delete files **H**.

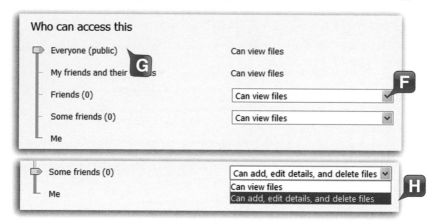

8. To add individuals to your list of people with access to your folder, type their email address into the **Enter a name or an email address:** text box **I**.

9. Hit **Enter** on your keyboard. Their name will appear under the text box with a control level settings pulldown **J**. Choose control level setting for each person you add.

10. Click **Save** **K**.

11. If you wish those who now have access to receive a notification, click **Send** in the **Send Notification for {Folder Name}** page. Click **Skip this** if you do not want to send a notification.

12. Your permissions will be updated and your approved colleagues will be able to access and edit your files. In Word, hit the **Refresh** button in the **Save to Windows Live SkyDrive** pane. You will see the folder moved to the **Shared Folders** heading and the **Shared with:** notification reflect your new settings 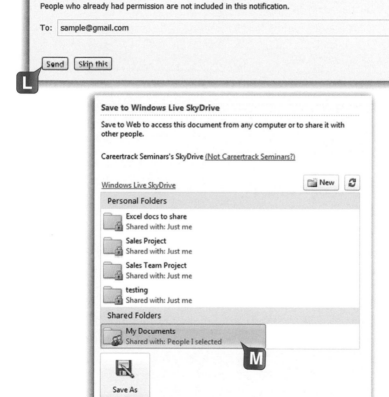.

63 | Invite Collaborators to View Your Shared Folders

Difficulty: ●●●○

PROBLEM You have created several documents and saved them to shared folders on your Windows Live SkyDrive. You want to send instructions to your Sales Team that will be reviewing and editing your documents. You need a way to tell them where to access the folders.

SOLUTION Send a notification with a link to the shared folders.

 What Microsoft Calls It: Send a Link

 Step-by-Step

1. Log in to your Windows Live account by following the first three steps in the *Share Your Document Using Windows Live SkyDrive* tip.

2. Hover over the name of the top-level folder that you have shared. A popup menu will appear **A**.

3. Click the **Share** dropdown menu, then click on **Send a link B**.

4. The **To:** text box will be pre-filled with individuals to whom you have already given access. You may remove people from the notification list by clicking the "x" beside their address **C** (this will not remove that person from the permissions). You may also add new people to the notification.

5. Click the **Require recipients to sign in with Windows Live ID** checkbox **D**. ⚠

6. Click **Send E**. An e-mail will be sent to each recipient in the **To:** list with a link to your shared folder **F**.

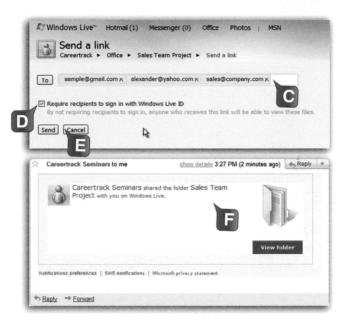

CONTINUE

Invite Collaborators to View Your Shared Folders   **233**

63

Invite Collaborators to View Your Shared Folders (continued)

Caution: If you do not click the **Require recipients to sign in with Windows Live ID** checkbox, anyone in your **To:** list will be able to view the files from the e-mail link, even if they have not been granted "can view files" persmissions.

Hot Tip: If you want to combine a link to your shared folder with personalized instructions, use the **Get a link** menu option from the **Share** dropdown Ⓖ. On the **Get a link** page, select the URL from the **Copy this link to share:** text box Ⓗ, then right-click to Copy (or use Ctrl+C). Paste the URL into an e-mail message of your own making with your instructions.

Quickest Click: You can **Send a Link**  directly from Word 2010. Go to the **Send Using E-mail** sub-tab under the **Save & Send** tab in the File menu. This will launch an e-mail message with the name of the file included in the subject line and a link to the document in the body of the text **J**. Fill in the addressees and your message, then click **Send**. Your recipients will need a Windows Live ID to access the document.

Create and Use Digital Signatures

Digital signatures are certifications of a document's authenticity. When sending important documents via e-mail or other online message service, a digital signature can provide some measure of certainty that a document has actually come from its alleged source and that it has not been altered since it was sent.

You can get a certificate from a certificate authority (a third party service online), but it is not free. To find out about third party certificates, choose Office, Finish, Add a Digital Signature, and then click Signature Services from the Office Marketplace. You can also self-certify a document, but this is not very secure and carries no legal authority. If you want to practice using digital signatures, though, a self-certificate will work..

Add a Digital Signature:

1. Click the **File** tab.

2. On the Info tab select **Protect Document** to open the dropdown.

3. Choose **Add a Digital Signature** .

4. If you do not have a third-party, digital signature file installed, a dialog box will offer to take you to Office Marketplace or to continue. Follow the prompts to either create your own or use a third party to obtain the digital ID.

Caution: If you are utilizing a digital signature for legal or organizational use, discuss your options with legal counsel to make sure that you are following proper procedure for liability purposes.

B | Keyboard Shortcuts

Keyboard Shortcut	Description

Common Tasks

Keyboard Shortcut	Description
CTRL+SHIFT+SPACEBAR	Create a nonbreaking space
CTRL+SHIFT+HYPHEN	Create a nonbreaking hyphen
CTRL+B	Bold text
CTRL+I	Italic text
CTRL+U	Underline Text
CTRL+SHFT+<	Decrease font size one value
CTRL+SHFT+>	Increase font size one value
CTRL+[	Shrink font size by 1 point
CTRL+]	Grow font size by 1 point
CTRL+SPACEBAR	Remove paragraph or character formatting
CTRL+C	Copy selected text or object
CTRL+X	Cut selected text or object
CTRL+ALT+V	Paste special
CTRL+SHFT+V	Paste formatting only
CTRL+Z	Undo the last action
CTRL+Y	Redo the last action
CTRL+SHFT+G	Open the Word Count dialog box

Document Shortcuts

Keyboard Shortcut	Description
CTRL+N	Create a new document
CTRL+O	Open a document
CTRL+W	Close a document
ALT+CTRL+S	Split the document window
ALT+SHIFT+C or ALT+CTRL+S	Remove the document window split
CTRL+S	Save a document
CTRL+F	Find – Open the Navigation task pane to search document
CTRL+PAGE UP	Move to previous browse object (set in browse options)
CTRL+PAGE DOWN	Move to next browse object (set in browse options)
CTRL+P	Print a document
ALT+CTRL+I	Switch to print preview

Keyboard Shortcut	Description
ALT+CTRL+M	Insert a comment
CTRL+SHIFT+E	Turn change tracking on or off
ALT+SHIFT+C	Close the Reviewing Pane if it is open

Editing Shortcuts

BACKSPACE	Delete one character to the left
CTRL+BACKSPACE	Delete one word to the left
DELETE	Delete one character to the right
CTRL+DELETE	Delete one word to the right

Function Keys

F1	Open Help or visit Microsoft Office.com
F2	Move text or graphics
F4	Repeat the last action
F5	Choose the Go To command (Home tab)
F6	Go to the next pane or frame
F7	Choose the Spelling command (Review tab)
F8	Extend a selection
F9	Update the selected fields
F10	Show KeyTips (see also: "The Magic ALT Key")
F11	Go to the next field
F12	Choose the Save As command

The "Magic" ALT Key

When you press the ALT key on your keyboard, letters appear on the ribbon. Clicking a letter launches the corresponding function. Unlike other keyboard shortcuts, ALT shortcut keys are pressed sequentially, not held down at once. This can be much faster than using the mouse.

Index